UP 2 YOU

ANDY STANLEY

WITH HEATH BENNETT

Multnomah® Publishers *Sisters, Oregon*

UP TO YOU

published by Multnomah Publishers, Inc.

© 2005 by Andy Stanley
International Standard Book Number: 1-59052-516-7

Unless otherwise indicated, Scripture quotations are from:
New American Standard Bible® © 1960, 1977, 1995 by the Lockman Foundation.
Used by permission.
Other Scripture quotations are from:
The Holy Bible, *English Standard Version* (ESV) © 2001 by Crossway Bibles, a division of Good
News Publishers. Used by permission. All rights reserved.
The Holy Bible, New International Version (NIV)
© 1973, 1984 by International Bible Society,
used by permission of Zondervan Publishing House

Multnomah is a trademark of Multnomah Publishers, Inc.,
and is registered in the U.S. Patent and Trademark Office.
The colophon is a trademark of Multnomah Publishers, Inc.

Printed in the United States of America

For information:
MULTNOMAH PUBLISHERS, INC. · 601 N. Larch St. · SISTERS, OR 97759

Library of Congress Cataloging-in-Publication Data
Stanley, Andy.
    Up 2 U / Andy Stanley with Heath Bennett.
        p. cm.
    Includes bibliographical references and index.
    ISBN 1-59052-516-7 (alk. paper)
    I. Christian life. I. Title: Up two you. II. Title: Up to you. III. Bennett, Heath.
IV. Title.
    BV4501.3.S733 2005
    248.4—dc22

                                    2005006383

05 06 07 08 09 10—10 9 8 7 6 5 4 3 2 1 0

CONTENTS

INTRODUCTION

IF ONLY...

Have you ever found yourself trying to justify something you really want to do but you're not sure you should? *But what's wrong with it?* you ask yourself. *What can it hurt?*

Or how about this one: *If it's not wrong, then it must be right. Right?*

You aren't alone. Most of us—no, *all* of us—have used this line of reasoning at some point in our lives to talk ourselves into making a questionable choice. These questions come up frequently during our teenage years and into adulthood when so many of life's decisions become *our* decisions and not Mom and Dad's anymore. And that's the way we want it, right? But these questions don't get any easier to answer as we get older. The choices are just different.

So what do you do when the answers aren't clear? When you want to do what's right, but the right choice is not so obvious. When you have to choose between *a* and *b*, but you're not sure what to do. *Should I stay home or go to the party? Should I say yes and go out with him or not? Should I have fries with that or a salad?* Questions that you deal with every week, many of which seem innocent but can have lasting repercussions.

So what is the answer? How can you know which direction to take, especially when both options seem right? It's hard, right?

Maybe you're asking the wrong questions.

I think I've found a better one.

Not just better. The *best*.

The great thing is, it's just one question.

Once you ask this question, then it's all up to you.

LOOKING BACK

We all make choices every day that determine what direction we are heading and where we're coming from. Sure, some things we have no control over, but too often we point a finger at other people for our own dumb mistakes when we should be pointing back at ourselves. We make a bad choice and we pay the consequences.

Maybe there's one particular incident or even a whole year of your life that you want to forget about, to wipe away. You want to forget about it, you try to forget about it. But the consequences are still there. And for some reason you keep making the same mistakes over and over.

And yet *your greatest regret could have been avoided had you asked yourself just one question and then acted on your conclusion.*

A bit strong?

To think that one question could radically change the outcome of your choices may seem ridiculous. But I truly believe that regardless of whether it is a single event you regret or an entire chapter of your life that you wish you could do over, had you evaluated your options by asking this single powerful question, you would have avoided what may be your greatest ongoing source of pain. As you move through the pages that follow, you may find that this one question could change the trajectory of your entire life.

In fact, I believe this question is so important, I call it the Best Question Ever.

It is a question I ask more than once every day. It is a question that guided me through my late twenties as a single man. It is a question that has served me well through sixteen incredible years of marriage. It is a question I have taught my three kids to ask about every option that comes their way. They know it is the lens through which we evaluate every decision we make as a family.

Over the past twenty years I have had the opportunity to teach this principle to thousands of middle-school and high school students. Many of them are adults now with children of their own. Letters, e-mails, and conversations assure me that the Best Question Ever continues to serve as a decision-making filter for scores of these young adults.

When I share this one question with adult audiences, the response is nearly always the same: "I wish I had heard this years ago." Translated: "I could have avoided some regret if only..."

The Best Question Ever serves as a lens through which you can evaluate your options. It is a filter that casts things in their actual light. It is a grid that provides context for every decision. It is a question that will give you a whole new perspective on your dating life, your friends, and your stuff. And it will shed some light on issues the Bible doesn't specifically address.

But the Best Question Ever is not always an easy question to ask. It can be a bit threatening. It exposes so much about our hearts and our motives that it is, well, it's just not an easy question to ask. That's just one more reason why it is the Best Question Ever.

LOOKING AHEAD

Here's where we're headed. The book is divided into six sections. First we're going to talk about why this question is so important, and then look one by one at the areas of your life that will benefit from asking this one question. Take your time and really think about each of these sections. Each piece of your future is up to you and no one else, so don't cheat yourself by skipping parts. At the end of these sections there will be some questions to help you look at how your life has been up to this point and where you *want* it to be. It really is up to you.

All right, it's time to get started. I hope you enjoy the book. More importantly, I hope this powerful question becomes a permanent part of your decision-making process. If you have the courage to ask it, your heavenly Father will use this simple question to guide and protect you in the days to come. And as you experience the difference this question makes, I think you will agree that it really is the Best Question Ever.

Andy Stanley

PART I

THE QUESTION

DUMB AND DUMBER
Finding Common Ground

If you're reading this, you and I have something in common. We have both done some really dumb stuff. Stuff we hope nobody ever finds out about. Stuff we wish we could forget. People we wish we had never gone out with, friends we wish we hadn't listened to, tests we wish we hadn't cheated on, words we wish we hadn't yelled at Mom and Dad. Places we shouldn't have hung out, things we shouldn't have seen, parties we should have declined when invited.

If you're like me, you look back and wonder, *How could I have been so foolish, so ignorant, so...dumb?* We should have known better. In most cases, we did know better, but we thought we could beat the odds. Despite what our gut and a couple of friends told us, we believed that we could control the outcome of our decisions. So we followed our hearts, listened to our emotions, and then let the chips fall where they may. And then we paid for it later. And now we wonder what in the world we were thinking.

Some of our decisions we wish we could unmake led to chapters of our lives we wish we could go back and un-live. Going out on a blind date is one thing. Carrying on a relationship with someone who doesn't have the same morals and values as you can hurt for a long time.

What's obvious now wasn't so obvious then. And what's obvious to us now may not be so obvious to everybody around us. Then you come across a friend who is about to make the same dumb mistake that you made. You know that guy is no good, or that crowd is bad news. You try to warn your friend, but she doesn't listen. Instead, she endures your tales of woe, thanks you for the unsolicited advice, and continues full speed ahead into the oncoming train. And you think back and wonder, *Could I have possibly been that naive? That stubborn? That foolish? That dumb?*

Yep.

POOR PLANNING

When we watch people we know—or strangers for that matter—make foolish decisions, it may seem as if they are intentionally trying to mess up their lives.

Having watched dozens of people methodically waste their lives, potential, and money, I've concluded that while nobody *plans* to mess up their life, the problem is that few of us *plan not to*. That is, we don't put the necessary safeguards in place to ensure a happy ending.

Nobody plans to have a baby before graduating high school.

Nobody plans on coming home the second semester of their sophomore year at college because they were better at going to parties than going to class.

Nobody plans to develop an addiction, but it happens. Why? A lack of necessary precaution.

Not looking ahead many times leads us right to where we weren't planning on going. Places we really didn't want to go.

The reality is that it is *up to you*. In many ways, where you end up at thirty or forty years old will be a direct result of the decisions you make now. Is there a way to avoid the traps that so many fall victim to?

Yep. There is one question you can ask that will provide the answer for you. Better yet, this question will help you stay out of the situations and circumstances that can rob you of your potential, your opportunities, and your future.

A MOST UNCOMFORTABLE QUESTION

And the Courage to Ask It

At the age of twenty-five I came across three verses in the Bible that totally changed the way I made decisions. I suddenly had a new filter through which to evaluate every opportunity, invitation, and relationship—everything I was asked to do, everything I was tempted to become a part of. I began to consider my whole life through this new grid, a grid that boiled down to asking one simple question.

The reason I consider it the best question ever is that it has the potential to *foolproof* every aspect of your life. It will give you a new perspective on your love life, your future, your finances, your friends, your schedule, everything. It will help you know where to draw the line morally, relation-ally, and ethically. Like a piercing light, this powerful question cuts through the fog surrounding so many of your decisions and enables you to see clearly.

And yet, as you are about to discover, it's not an easy question to ask. It's not that the words are difficult to say. It's just that the question exposes so much about your heart and your motives that it is, well, it's just not an easy question to ask. It's like walking out of a dark building on a sunny day—there is something about this question that will make you want to retreat to the shadows where your eyes have already adjusted. Like direct sunlight to the unshielded eye, this question can be extremely uncomfortable.

Here's why.

THE ART OF SELF-DECEPTION

You see, in addition to making the occasional dumb deci-sion, you and I have something else in common: We are good at deceiving ourselves. Really good.

Self-deception comes naturally to me. I can make a bad decision look and sound like a great decision with one hand tied behind my back. I can make a poor choice of how to use my time and make it sound like a much needed "outlet." I've made poor relationship decisions sound like ministry opportunities. I've missed countless workouts under the guise of "I need my rest." I've rationalized gallons of ice cream with the phrase "Everybody needs to live a little," as if ice cream adds to the quality of life. I've wasted massive amounts of time doing all kinds of things that seemed important but had no cumulative value. And given enough time, I can even find a Bible verse or two to support my foolishness.

Every kind of addiction begins with similar self-deception.

"This won't hurt anybody."

"I'll only do it once."

"I haven't had any for a week."

"I'll be careful."

"I can handle it."

"I can quit whenever I want to."

Sound familiar? Chances are, you don't have to think past last week to come up with a bad decision or two that you talked yourself into. Probably some of your greatest regrets started with choices that you convinced yourself were good ones. But in fact you were actually robbing yourself. Your bad choices ended up costing you relationally, financially, and maybe even spiritually.

And the strange thing is, most of the time we are fully aware of the game we're playing. The fact that we have to give ourselves a reason or excuse at all ought to tip us off. Think about it. You don't have to go through a series of mental gymnastics to convince yourself that it's a good idea to eat a serving or two of vegetables every day. You never have to rationalize why you ought to exercise, study for a test, or avoid bad company. You just know. You don't sit around looking for reasons to do the right thing; it's the bad decisions that require creative reasoning.

READING THE GAUGES

The reason this question is so uncomfortable to ask is because we are so good at deceiving ourselves. This question exposes how lame our excuses really are. It reveals our true intent. It tears down the walls that we hide behind to excuse our bad choices. It dismantles the arguments we use to keep the truth at arm's length.

All of which is fine if you really want to do what is right. But this little question can become a nuisance on those occasions when, instead of trying to make a right decision, you are trying to make a decision right.

Say, what? You know, those times that don't really seem to be a "wrong" decision, but it's not obviously "right" either. We do our best to make the decision right because it is what we want to do. On those occasions this one question has the potential to irritate as well as illuminate. Because of that, it is very important for you to pay close attention to your emotional response to the Best Question Ever. Your reaction to this dynamic little question will tell you a great deal about yourself. And this is one lesson you cannot afford to miss.

THE SLIPPERY SLOPE
WHY EVERYBODY GOES THERE

OK, so now that I've got you interested in what we're talking about here, let me take you to those verses that changed forever the way I make decisions. We find them in the apostle Paul's first-century letter to Christians residing in the city of Ephesus. You know it as the book of Ephesians.

Paul starts his letter by reminding his readers who they are in Christ. By being adopted into God's family, they have a new identity and there are some serious benefits that come with being "in Christ." Beginning in chapter four, however, Paul turns a corner.

He begins the second half of the book with this plea: "[I]

urge you to walk in a manner worthy of the calling to which you have been called" (Ephesians 4:1, ESV). In other words, live your life in a way that reflects the changes God has made in you. Or as a friend of mine is fond of saying, "Don't live the way you used to live. After all, you are not the person you used to be."

From there Paul launches into one of the most practical sections in the Bible. He talks about everything from sex to marriage to alcohol. He gives instructions on what is permissible to talk about, think about, and even laugh about. The entire discussion is intense and thorough and, frankly, somewhat overwhelming.

GIMME TRACTION

Paul goes so far as to suggest that we become imitators of God! My gut response? *Yeah, right. Not in this lifetime.*

It's not that Paul's list of lofty standards isn't worth striving toward. It's just that I know me. I'm not that good, that consistent, that disciplined. Besides, just about everything in Paul's list runs directly against what I see going on around me every day. So let's face it, I'm not going to get any support out in the real world.

Read Ephesians 4 and 5 for yourself. It's an incredible catalog of virtues and values, the kind of stuff parents preach to their children all the time. The kind of stuff that children end up challenging when they hit their teen years. But is it realistic? Can anybody really pull it off? At first glance, I don't think so.

The good news is that Paul anticipates our frustration. So he incorporates into this intimidating list of what-to-do an invaluable *how-to-do-it*. Specifically, he unveils an approach to life that, if embraced, will set us up for success as we attempt to live out the values he has listed. And it is from this short but powerful piece of instruction that we derive the Best Question Ever.

Here's what Paul writes:

Therefore be careful how you walk, not as unwise men but as wise, making the most of your time, because the days are evil. So then do not be foolish, but understand what the will of the Lord is. (Ephesians 5:15–17)

Life changing, huh?

No? Okay, let's break it down.

Paul starts off with a big transition word, a word loaded with implications:

Therefore...

As a mentor of mine was fond of saying, whenever you see a *therefore*, you gotta ask, "What's it *there for*?" On this particular occasion, "therefore" connects all the stuff Paul is telling us we *need* to do with his explanation of *how* to do it.

It's as if he is saying, "If the values and practices I've talked about—as overwhelming as they may seem—are things you desire to embrace, if you want to live life on an entirely different plane, then here's what you need to do."

Then Paul reveals the principle that gives all of us wannabe Christ followers the traction we need to live out what, at times, seems out of reach:

...be careful how you walk...

Or to turn it around, *Don't be careless how you walk.* In other words, following Christ is not a casual endeavor. It requires extreme caution. If we are serious about living out the values the Bible teaches, we must watch our step. After all, we know from experience how easy it is to stumble.

Then without so much as a pause, Paul discloses the criterion by which we are to measure and judge every one of our choices. In the six words that follow, we are given the standard, the yardstick by which we are to assess our relational, spiritual, and moral decisions. Get out your highlighter.

...not as unwise men but as wise...

Okay, so you've gotten this far without even knowing what the question is. Are you ready for the Best Question Ever? The question that can help us avoid the dumb mistakes we so often make? Here it is:

What is the wise thing to do?

Wait a minute. That's it? How could that possibly be the best question ever? How could that simple question be the key to consistency in our walk with Christ? How could this question help us to avoid the pitfalls waiting ahead on the road of life? To understand the real potency of this question, we need to examine the way we're used to evaluating our options.

WE'RE ASKING THE WRONG QUESTIONS

Typically when making choices, we run our options and opportunities through a more generic and far less helpful grid. There are several variations, but basically the question we ask ourselves is this: *Is there anything wrong with it?*

The assumption is that if there is nothing *wrong* with what we're doing, it must be okay. If it is not illegal, immoral, or potentially fatal, then it qualifies as a live option, right? Biblically speaking, if there is not a "Thou shalt not" associated with it, then it's safe to assume it qualifies as a "Thou certainly shalt if thou please."

Unfortunately, that kind of thinking sets us up for another question that we rarely ask out loud or even allow to surface to the level of conscious thought. Yet if we are honest, this is a question that drives far too many of our choices. It goes something like this: *How close can I get to the line between right and wrong without actually doing something wrong?* The Christian version goes like this: *How close can I get to sin without actually sinning?*

This is a question every teenage guy has asked in some way at some point in his dating career. It's a question everyone on a diet asks every day. It's a question every student has considered when taking the test they didn't study for.

But it doesn't stop there. Inevitably, once we have come this far we find ourselves asking, *How far over the line between right and wrong can I go without experiencing consequences?* In other words, what can I touch, taste, see, or experience without having some kind of lasting negative outcome. How far can I go with my girlfriend before it becomes "sex"? How far over the speed limit can I drive without getting pulled over? How many drinks can I have without getting drunk (or getting caught)?

It starts with a simple and logical question, *Is there anything wrong with it?* But then it becomes like a waterslide covered in grease. You can't stop it once it starts, and then you end with a different question: *How did I get myself into this?*

Ever happened to you? If you're breathing, I think it has.

DAMAGE CONTROL

It's a question I have heard dozens of times. I've asked myself the same question a dozen times or more: *How in the world could someone as smart as me get myself into*—well, it's really none of your business what I've gotten myself into. Let's talk about you, or Chip.

Chip is one of the most talented guys I've ever met. He walked into our student ministry one Wednesday night and I knew immediately that this kid had potential. Everybody loved Chip. But not unlike a lot of guys his age, Chip enjoyed walking on the edge. He was just careful enough to stay out of any real trouble, but curious enough to get close to stuff that could hurt him.

The first time I taught the material in this book, Chip was there. Over the years he had heard a lot of good teaching from several great communicators. He was at every youth camp. He even participated in two mission trips. But in spite of all that he continued to live right on the line between what was permissible and what could be painful. As long as it wasn't "wrong," as long as it was "legal," as long as the consequences were "minor," Chip could rationalize anything. He wanted to go as far as he could go without getting caught or getting hurt.

Chip disappeared in the middle of his senior year. I don't mean he vanished into thin air. He just quit coming around.

The next time I saw Chip, he was twenty-six. He showed up one morning at church. He asked if we could get together and so we did. For two hours he poured out his story—alcohol, DUIs, community service, a lost scholarship, relationships gone bad, thousands of dollars in debt, dropped out of college…you get the picture. Chip hadn't planned for anything like this to happen. But he had neglected to plan *not* to mess up his life.

Every bad choice Chip had made could have been avoided if only he had asked the Best Question Ever. His was not an IQ problem. As is the case with most people, his nightmare began with the assumption that he could dance on the edge of moral, relational, and professional disaster and beat the odds. But he was wrong. Eventually Chip crossed a few lines that made it very easy to cross others.

Chip is now in the process of rebuilding his life. But he's digging himself out of a pretty deep hole.

The moral of the story is, just because there isn't a "Thou shalt not" attached to a situation it does not necessarily mean it is a "Thou shalt." Just because it seems right, doesn't always make it so.

As a pastor, I've heard more than my fair share of heart-breaking stories. Yet every bad decision I have ever heard about could have been avoided if the person had simply stopped and asked the Best Question Ever. Bad relation-ships, unwanted pregnancies, substance abuse, bad debts—all could have been avoided by using this one simple question.

Like a good father, God wants what's best for each of us. So He has given us a standard that goes beyond what your friends, MTV, or even your brain tells you is okay. He has given us a question that helps us to live out the values that lead to what Jesus referred to as an abundant life (see John 10:10). Not a barely-get-by life. Not a life of regret. *An abundant life.*

But the question He gave us is not, *Is there anything wrong with it?* The question is, *Is it the wise thing to do?* To foolproof your life, you must ask it of every invitation, every opportunity, every relationship.

What is the wise thing for me to do?

Think back for a moment to your biggest regret. That event or chapter of your life you wish you could go back and undo or relive. What was the decision you wish you could reverse? The relationship you wish you could do over? Can you see how some or all of what you regret could have been avoided if you had asked and applied this question to the situation?

CLIMATE CONTROL
IT'S A MYTH

God never intended for us to live a life that pushes the limits of what's permissible, what's acceptable, or what's not prosecutable. By living this way, our lives are driven by the question, *How close can I get to sin without sinning?* Now *there's* a standard.

Instead, we are to look hard at every situation and consider our options through the lens of wisdom. Every choice should be tested with the simple question, *What is the wise thing to do?* This is what Paul means when he tells us to be careful how we live.

Speaking of Paul, in the last chapter we cut him off in mid-sentence, so let's pick up where we left off. After telling his audience to walk wisely, Paul goes on to say:

...making the most of your time, because the days are evil.

Evil days? What does he mean by evil? To some, evil is the music you just downloaded on your iPod. To others, it is the Satan worshiper who wears black and has a pentagram sticker on his car. Well, after looking at what life was like in Ephesus, it is pretty clear what Paul is talking about. In Ephesus, sex was everywhere. I'm talking Spring Break on steroids. Prostitutes were rampant in the pagan churches, and sex was even part of their "worship" services. Drunkenness was encouraged as well. No wonder the temple was always packed.

Apparently, some of the Christians in Ephesus were being drawn back into their old ways. Why settle for a sermon when you can...never mind. Anyway, they were attempting to blend the old with the new; they were blurring the lines. And some were beginning to suffer the consequences of their actions. So Paul goes right to the heart of the matter.

"You can't be careless!" he warns. "You don't live in a world that is morally neutral. If you don't put up your guard and keep it up, you will get sucked in!"

ASLEEP AT THE WHEEL

We don't live in a morally neutral world, either. Every day we come face to face with a world of sexuality, greed, and pride.

Our television, movies, and music tell us to live it up and indulge ourselves in whatever feels good at the moment.

These are evil days. You don't have to go looking for trouble. Trouble finds you. It is on every street corner, on every page of just about every magazine. Trouble is dripping from every billboard. Trouble drives across our television screens and calls to us from our computers.

Free phones!

Click here for a private viewing!

No payments for one full year!

Try it for 30 days risk-free!

Girls Gone Wild!

Most Americans are overweight and overleveraged. We eat too much and spend too much. By far, the biggest online moneymaker is pornography. Consider this: American men spend hundreds of millions of dollars every year to look at pictures of women on their computer screens. *Hundreds of millions of dollars.*

We do not live in a morally neutral society. The world we live in is much like the grassy area outside my basement door where I let my black lab, Shadow, out to do her business every night. If you are not "careful how you walk," you will step in it.

All right, so that's a little gross, but you get the point. Like the Ephesians in Paul's day, we live in some rough times. The days are evil. If you don't pay attention, you will end up paying a price for your carelessness. If you aren't intentionally cautious, you may end up falling into a behavior or habit you once thought of as wrong. You could find yourself facing the severe consequences of a very bad decision, just because you didn't ask yourself one simple question.

THIS IS YOUR WAKE-UP CALL

So right now, you might be thinking about putting the book down. Please don't! I know the question is irritating. I know it can get your blood boiling. After all, it forces you to face up to what you have spent years of time and energy trying to ignore. It's like an alarm clock for your heart, a wake-up call for your soul. It's irritating, but necessary. Perhaps it was the universal propensity to wear out our snooze buttons that drove the apostle Paul to continue with these words:

So then do not be foolish...

If punctuation had been available in the first century, I imagine that this phrase may have come with double excla-mation points. "Do not be foolish" is a polite way of saying, "Don't be a fool! Don't look at this world like it is safe."

Then Paul commands us to do something that on the surface appears to be impossible.

...but understand what the will of the Lord is.

You can't command someone to understand something, can you? Your parents have tried it for years, to no avail.

I had a Greek teacher in college who would have us come up to the front of the room and translate out loud for the class. There I was with my paperback copy of *The Iliad*, standing in front of my peers and bluffing my way through some incident in the Trojan War, filling in the gaps with my own editorial comments. When it became evident that I was no longer translating but merely telling the story from memory, the teacher would stop me and say, "Mr. Andy, I don't think you are reading." Busted.

"You are right, Mrs. Cuntz," I would reply. "I can't translate it."

Her reply was always the same. "Yes, you can! Now translate it for us."

"I really can't."

"Yes, you can. Now translate."

She would always insist that we understood more than we did, as if her insistence would somehow increase our capacity for the Greek language. It never did. Eventually she would allow us to give up and return to our seats. I always felt like Mrs. Cuntz took my ignorance personally. Funny, it never seemed to bother me. Oh, well.

Whenever I read Paul's admonition to "understand what the will of the Lord is," I always think of Mrs. Cuntz exhorting us to *understand* Plato. Both seem like a waste of time. You can rah-rah an athlete to perform better, but you can't rah-rah someone into knowing something they don't know.

So what is Paul's point? Why didn't he say, "*Discover* what the will of the Lord is"? Or perhaps, "*Obey* the will of the Lord"? We could move on either of those. But why *understand*?

FACE-OFF

When Paul tells the church in Ephesus to understand God's will, he is really saying, "face up" to what you know you should do. We're all good at fooling ourselves. So Paul, leveraging the grammar of his day, reaches off the page, grabs us by the collar, yanks us up close, and shouts, "Quit playing games! Quit pretending, quit rationalizing, ask the question, and embrace the answer!" This is Paul's final attempt to get us to admit what we know in our hearts to be true—to admit that we generally know already what God would have us do.

One reason we don't admit certain things to ourselves is that it helps us to avoid the guilt that naturally follows from not doing what we know we should. This is why most Americans eat so unhealthily. It's not *just* a lack of discipline. Americans haven't really faced up to the reality of what the foods they eat are doing to their bodies. How do I know? Because I've seen how quickly the diet changes once someone has had a brush with cancer or heart disease. Lumps, clogs, and shortness of breath force a person to face up to what he or she has refused to acknowledge for years. And the revelation leads to death-defying discipline.

But lifestyle changes don't happen until an individual faces the facts. It is not until a person acknowledges the truth and quits lying to himself that something positive takes place. And once someone has turned the corner mentally, it's amazing how quickly that person is able to break unhealthy habits and begin new routines.

Every person I know who has undergone this kind of transformation after a health scare says the same thing: "I should have made these changes years ago." Translated: "For years I refused to face up to what I knew in my heart was true."

Teen pregnancy can have the same effect. Or getting an *F* on your report card. Or having your license revoked. And perhaps that's what it will take. There is something out there somewhere that has the ability to get your attention. Unfortunately, that something may scar you as well as scare you. You may be left with limited options and reduced opportunities. So why let things go that far? Why not face up now to what you know in your heart your heavenly Father wants you to do?

Why not start asking the Best Question Ever?

STEMMING THE TIDE
AVOIDING THE UNDERTOW

When I was a kid we lived in Miami. Every summer we would pull our eighteen-foot travel trailer to Naples, Florida, for a week of vacation. If you've been to Naples lately, you know the waterfront is lined with condos and hotels. But in 1968 there was nothing but miles of empty beach. So my dad would actually pull out onto the beach and drive along the tree line where the sand was firm. Then we would drive for miles until we found a suitable place to set up camp.

Although I was in elementary school at the time, I still have a vivid memory of something that happened during one of our weeks on the beach. That particular year the under-tow was ferocious. It wasn't dangerous, in the sense that the undertow might pull you out to sea, but it would carry you down the beach in no time. I still remember playing in the water, looking back toward the shore, and our trailer not being there! Why would my parents move the campsite? Well, of course, they hadn't moved—I was forty yards down the beach from where I had stepped into the water. It was the undertow.

Well, after a couple of days of looking out from the trailer and wondering where his kids had drifted off to, my dad came up with a novel idea. He gathered about twenty coconuts and made a neat little cannonball-like stack about thirty yards down the beach from where our trailer was parked. The coconuts were to serve as a reference point. Once we drifted past the coconuts, we were to get out of the water, walk back to the point where we were even with the trailer, and then we could swim again. And it worked.

You may already know where I'm going with this. Like the undertow at Naples, culture has a way of subtly sweeping us beyond healthy moral, ethical, and financial limits. That accounts for the times when we have looked up and said, "Who moved the trailer?" Or rather, "How did I get myself into this situation?" When everything around you is drifting along at the same rate, it's easy to be fooled into thinking that you're standing still. Without a stationary reference point, it is impossible to ascertain where you are, where you aren't, and where you ought to be.

So let's stake out some stationary reference points.

Specifically, we are going to ask the Best Question Ever

in three different ways. Not three different questions, just three different perspectives. Looking at three parts of your life will help in knowing exactly how you should answer the question.

Here we go.

LOOKING BACK

Poet and philosopher George Santayana once said, "Those who cannot remember the past are condemned to repeat it." (Now I remember why I am not a poet or a philosopher.) Let me try and restate this for the rest of us normal people: "If you messed up in the past and didn't learn from it, you are probably gonna mess up again."

It's not very catchy, but you get the point.

We have about 1500 teenagers in our student ministry every week. They come each week with the same issues teenagers all over the country are dealing with—bad relationships, broken relationships, no relationships. But at the end of any dating relationship or friendship, they always ask the same question: "Why does every relationship end the same way?" In almost every case the answer is, "Because every relationship started the same way."

I wonder if Dr. Phil is looking for a cohost?

Not only did every relationship start the same way, they were conducted the same way as well. So consequently, they all ended the same way. We mistakenly think that swapping boyfriends or girlfriends will itself guarantee us a different kind of relationship. It's the same line of thinking that leads us to buy new tennis rackets, golf clubs, and baseball bats—as if new equipment will somehow compensate for a poor swing. Expensive wheels on your car do not make you a better driver. A new guitar does not guarantee better music. And bad relational habits are not corrected by starting a new relationship.

So the Best Question Ever needs to be asked with an eye to the rearview mirror: *In light of your past experience, what is the wise thing to do?*

HISTORY LESSONS

I love history. I hated history *class,* but I love history. A few years ago I had an opportunity to go to England. Talk about history! There are buildings still standing there that are older than our country! Here we do a great job of knocking down old things, but the English just turn them into tourist attractions. It was amazing to walk through ancient castles and hear stories of kings and queens, knights and fair maidens. Stories of the rise and fall of great leaders, many of whom fell because of bad choices they made, resulting in the loss of many lives and many heads—sometimes their own. Rulers of England came and went, but the most successful were those who learned from the mistakes of their predecessors.

Each of us has a history—a history we can either learn from or ignore. We can either learn from our past to better our future, or we can continue to make the same mistakes again and again.

Before making any decision, consider your past. Chances are, there are places you have no business visiting because of your history—places that may have little impact on the average person, but then the average person doesn't share your experience with those environments. Perhaps there are certain types of people you have no business spending time with—because being around them triggers something devilish in you.

Every year we see students return from summer camp, all gung-ho about living differently and making a difference in the lives of their friends. It would be easy to write it off as a "camp experience" that will soon wither when they get home, but many of these students sincerely want to make the right choices when they get back to school. But then we ask the big question: "What are you willing to change when you get back?" Many times we get the same response: "What do I need to change? I'll just try harder. I'm really going to do it this time." Sadly enough, most of these students fail.

Why should they fail? It's not that they aren't sincere. It's because they aren't willing to make the break from the people and activities that caused them to struggle in the first place. A relationship that needed to end, parties that needed to be avoided, friends that were negative influences. They aren't willing to consider what hindered them in their past so that their future could be a lot brighter.

I know teenagers who stopped dating for a season of their lives because they struggled physically. Is dating wrong? I hope not. If so, I was sinning for months before I asked my wife to marry me. But for many, their past experiences with dating should caution them as to who, how, and when they pursue dating.

I know girls who stopped going to parties, guys who got rid of their Internet service, all because of the Best Question Ever. These are young men and women who had the courage to face up to God's will for their lives. They knew that their past set them up for failure if they did not take drastic steps. So in light of their past experience, they did the wise thing. The unusual thing. The extreme thing.

GUT CHECK

What about you? In light of your past experience, what is the wise thing for *you* to do?

What is the wise thing to do in your dating life?

On your weekends?

With your friendships?

Where are you set up to fail because of something in your past? Perhaps it was something you had no control over, yet there it is, reaching into your current experience and wreaking havoc with your choices. Does the way you were raised predispose you to an area of temptation to which most people seem immune? If so, admit it. Own up to it. Don't be content with merely doing the right thing.

Do the wise thing.

SEASONAL WISDOM
BIDING YOUR TIME

So is that it? If I take a look at my past, it can help me make decisions about my future. That's all there is to it, right? Not quite. We live in the here and now. What is going on in our lives today should influence every decision we make. We stated earlier that we need to look at three parts of our lives before we can fully understand the Best Question Ever. Let's take a look at the second part.

The question goes something like this:

In light of my current circumstances, what is the wise thing to do?

Life is seasonal. Today's sorrow will be replaced by tomorrow's joy. Today's anger will probably be tempered with tomorrow's perspective. Today's worry will be replaced by tomorrow's concerns. As Jesus taught, each day has its own worries. If we are not careful, we will allow the pressure, fears, and circumstances of today to drive us to make decisions we will regret tomorrow.

That being the case, you owe it to yourself, and to the people you love, to take your current emotions and state of mind into account when making decisions. I don't know about you, but most of my apologies stem from my propensity to react to the moment. When the moment has passed, I discover I have overreacted and hurt someone in the process. I can't begin to remember all of the e-mails I wish I could unsend—I know that if I had waited even twenty-four hours, my response would have been much different. Consequently, there would have been far less residual damage. When I'm mad, I've learned that the wise thing for me to do is NOTHING. Just wait.

BEYOND THE MOMENT

But this angle on the Best Question Ever goes beyond the moment. What's wise in this season of life may be unwise in the next. And vice versa.

This is true in almost every avenue of life. Even our government understands this principle. This is why you must reach a certain age before obtaining a driver's license or voting or, in many states, getting married. Is there anything magical about the ages that were determined by our lawmakers? Nope. An age was determined by a group of officials elected by the people to help us find a "wise" time for young people to become involved in these activities. The assumption being that, on average, people have matured and are properly prepared by the time they reach the designated age.

It is important for every one of us to take a close look at our stage of life at this moment and ask ourselves this question: "Is it wise for me to be involved in this right now?" If not, does that mean it will never be wise for us to be involved in it? Absolutely not. But we could be robbing our future if we aren't willing to stop now and at least ask ourselves the Best Question Ever.

No Decision

Dating is an activity at the forefront of nearly every single person's life. If you're not dating, people want to know what is wrong with you. If you're dating the wrong girl, what is wrong with you? If you broke up with the guy everybody thought was "Mr. Right," what is wrong with you? Among the students at our church, this is a hot topic. Our small groups spend more time talking about guy/girl relationships than any other subject. The difficult thing about discussing dating is that the experience can vary wildly from person to person.

Sure, there are some core principles that we all need to live by—we're going to look at some of these later in the book—but many of our decisions will be based in part on our own past and present. Past relationships, recent struggles, and prior failures can provide some direction for how we approach dating in the future. In fact, if a student has struggled emotionally or physically in a recent relationship, I recommend that they take a break from dating for a while. Because right now, they're an ideal candidate for the same kind of hurt and heartache they've just emerged from. They need time to refocus and rethink how they approach relationships with the opposite sex.

In fact, many such students have opted out of dating totally. Are they more "spiritual" than those who have chosen to date again? Not at all. They've simply taken into consideration their past and their present and made the tough call to protect their future. They are seeking what is the wise thing for them to do.

LOOK AROUND

So in light of what's going on in your life right now, what is the wise thing for you to do? As you consider your frame of mind, your emotional state, and even your stage of life, what is the wise thing to do? As you consider your current responsibilities and commitments, things that a year from now may not be a factor, what is the wise thing to do? As you examine the current status of your friendships, what is the wise thing to do?

Life is seasonal. What is appropriate today may be completely inappropriate a month from now. What is foolish today may be prudent tomorrow. It is not enough to determine what is legal, permissible, or even practical. As a Christ-follower you have been called to approach life with a different standard. So you must ask, "For me, in light of my past experience and my current season of life, what is the wise thing to do?"

LOOKING AHEAD
CREATING YOUR
PREFERRED FUTURE

The Best Question Ever will provide you with the greatest insight when you ask it from three different angles. Again, each form of the question will provide you with a unique perspective on your options and decisions. Here's the final version of the question:

In light of my future hopes and dreams, what is the wise thing to do?

As a young man or woman it's sometimes tough to think about your future. You want to live for *now*. You want to experience life to the fullest before you get out into the real world and have to pay bills, change diapers, and buy a minivan. And you're right. You do need to live life to the fullest. But the problem is that many young people have fallen for the lie—the lie that tells you not to be concerned about how the decisions you make now will affect your future. The lie that says if it's not somewhat risky or even dangerous then it's got to be boring.

If I were to ask you where you envision yourself in ten years financially, you could come up with an answer. You have some idea of what that should look like. You might not even have a job yet, but that doesn't change the fact that you envision yourself bringing in the cash one day. You may not have a plan for getting there, but you almost certainly have a mental picture of what you want the cash flow to be like in your future. We all have certain hopes and dreams for the future. We may lack a plan, but we certainly have dreams and expectations.

DREAM WRECKERS

The truth is, most people's dreams don't come true. I don't know too many *adults* who are living their dream. And while it is true that the twists and turns of life can reshape our future, that is not the primary reason people are robbed of their dreams. We rob ourselves. We rob ourselves when we make decisions in the moment with no thought of how these decisions will impact our future.

This is easy to see in others. But somehow the person in the mirror is always the exception, or so we think.

You know people who have robbed themselves of their

preferred future. Too many bad relationships, too much partying, gone too far with her boyfriend, listening to too many voices in his ear. You know the drill. Just take a look at the next *E! True Hollywood Story* to see people who have had their hopes and dreams washed away by indulging instead of thinking. We've all watched somebody we care about trade his or her dreams for a moment, a weekend, a habit, a promise, or a kiss.

As a parent I am constantly urging my kids to make today's decisions in light of tomorrow's hopes and dreams. The future is what brings today's choices into proper focus. Making choices with the end in mind goes a long way toward ensuring a happy ending.

Today's decisions must be evaluated in light of how they will impact and shape tomorrow. Short of winning the lottery, your financial future will be determined by today's financial decisions. The health of your marriage tomorrow will be determined by the dating decisions you make today. The nature of your relationship with your parents once you move out hinges in large part on the decisions you and your parents make while you're still living at home.

I was reminded of the significance of this principle recently as I listened to a brokenhearted father describe his failed attempts to reconnect with his adult daughter. He could not understand why she refused to return his calls or accept his gifts. She was now married and had a little girl of her own. In her father's words, she was "depriving him" of his rights to be the grandfather he had always dreamed of being.

From where he stood, she had shut him out of her life for good, and with no justification. He was devastated.

But that wasn't the whole story.

When his daughter turned twelve, this man had an affair with an employee. His daughter was with her mom the night she spotted his car in a motel parking lot at the edge of town. This twelve-year-old girl saw her father come out of the room with his girlfriend in tow. She endured the humiliation that accompanied the divorce proceedings, and then she didn't hear from her father for fifteen years.

As much as I empathized with a father who wanted a relationship with his only daughter, I couldn't help but think, *You did this to yourself. You robbed yourself of the joy of seeing your daughter graduate from high school. You missed the once-in-a-lifetime opportunity to give her away at her wedding. You weren't there for the birth of your grand-daughter.* One stupid, irresponsible decision robbed him of what could have been and what should have been.

Who knows when his tendency toward promiscuity began. Maybe it was when he was in high school and found himself struggling to commit to a relationship. Maybe it was when he was in college where one-night stands became an everyday part of his life. Or maybe it was when he took that first peek at those forbidden websites, the ones that portray sex as merely an activity instead of an expression of intimacy. We don't know what led him to that motel room, but whatever it was completely shattered his dreams.

But he wasn't the only person whose dreams wouldn't come true. His daughter certainly didn't imagine growing up without her father. His wife certainly didn't dream of becoming a single mom. His decision derailed the dreams of everyone who was close to him. The shrapnel of his choices wounded everyone who loved him. In a moment, the future was changed forever. Nobody's dreams would come true.

Future Tense, Common Sense

Asking the Best Question Ever helps us to see that the choices that impact our future really are up to us. It reveals areas of our lives that would go unnoticed without asking the question and honestly answering it. The fog of our future is cleared and we are forced to deal with what could be and what should be. Still, some will retreat back to the same reasoning that first led them astray: *I'm not doing anything wrong. People do it all the time. I'm not hurting anyone. I can handle it. There's no law against it. Nobody's going to find out. Nothing's going to happen.*

Recently, the director of our student ministry asked each of our high school students to write a letter to his or her future spouse. The response was amazing. For most of the students this was the first time they had given their undivided attention to what they were looking forward to relationally. In a defining moment, it dawned on these young people how their current behavior would be either an investment in or a deterrent to that future relationship.

Following the letter-writing exercise, the leaders enacted a mock wedding, and our students were transported to an event so far in the future that it seemed to have no connection to the realities of their everyday lives. But in that moment, when they were fast-forwarded to a marriage altar, with all it represents, the casual decisions of adolescence took on extraordinary meaning. Suddenly, they realized that their tomorrows would, in fact, be shaped by today. The decisions made at thirteen could sculpt what life looked like at thirty-one.

The students were not the only ones moved by this exercise. Our adult leaders were impacted as well. But as you can imagine, their reaction was somewhat different from that of the students. Their response: "I wish someone had helped me to stop and think about my decisions based on how they would affect me in the future." Most of us had someone in our lives who tried. But we were seventeen and knew everything.

But the fact that the adults would feel that way should tell you something very important about all of us: Our lives would be better today if we had been asking the Best Question Ever along the way. We might be closer to living our dreams if we had guarded them more closely.

Is it too late to begin viewing today through the lens of tomorrow? I don't think so. Chances are, you've got plenty of tomorrows left.

So that settles it, right? From now on you will gauge the appropriateness of every option by your hopes and dreams for tomorrow. Every time there is a decision to make, you will reflexively stop and ask, "In light of my future hopes and dreams, what is the wise thing to do?" And then you will do it!

End of story. No need to finish this book.

MAYBE NOT

It's not that simple, is it? Or is it? Seems strange that we would digest this information and then turn right around and resist the obvious.

Isn't it ironic that at this very moment you are seriously contemplating a decision that has the potential to chip away at your preferred future, and yet you are leaning hard in that direction, rehearsing the same old worn-out excuses? You know which ones I'm talking about. The ones you've been using since junior high. The ones that cleared the way for you to do things you now wish you hadn't. Things you have never shared with your closest friends. Things you hope your parents never discover. Decisions you are ashamed of. Choices that, to this day, cast a shadow over the good things that have come your way. Options that, if avoided, would have paved the way for your dreams to come true.

Sorry to be so hard on you. It's just that I know my own tendency to deny this truth in the face of overwhelming evidence to the contrary. As I said earlier, it's easy to see how this principle has played out in the lives of others while ignoring its relevance in our own lives. We are indeed professionals in the art of deceiving ourselves.

So let's get specific. In light of what kind of home and family you want to have in ten years, what decisions are you making today to protect that? What choices are you willing to make to protect your future spouse from unwanted and unneeded hurt?

Many of you reading this will one day go to college. Some of you are already there. Are you making decisions today that will ensure your admission to a great school and/or keep you enrolled there? How about your relationships? What path are your friends leading you down? Are your friends concerned more about you or what they can get from you?

In light of where you want to be in your relationship with God in five years, are you doing what's necessary to create and maintain a habit of feeding yourself spiritually? Are you prioritizing time alone with God, or do the snooze button and the telephone get in the way?

It would be nice to go back and, knowing what we know now, relive sixth and seventh grade. Or at least redo last semester. But we can't. We get only one shot at each season of life. Whether or not we learn anything from the experience will become evident in the seasons that follow.

So what have you learned? More to the point, are you willing to face up to God's will for your life? Are you ready to acknowledge what you know in your heart is true? Are you prepared to ask the Best Question Ever and follow through? You can take a giant step toward protecting your future. In light of your future hopes and dreams, what is the wise thing to do?

WHERE DOES IT HURT?

For just a moment, let's pretend that no one, including God, can read your mind. Better yet, let's imagine that five minutes from now you will be able to erase your next five minutes' worth of thoughts. In other words, let's create some space for unfiltered thinking. You will not be accountable to anyone, including yourself, for the thoughts you are about to entertain.

If you can go with this for just a minute, you will be free to admit to yourself anything you want without feeling like you have to do anything about it. Because in five minutes you will be able to erase any incriminating thoughts that you allow yourself to think. With me?

Okay, let's do a little probing. Remember, you are free to admit to yourself anything you want. No action will be required.

As you evaluate where you are relationally, morally, and spiritually, what would you do differently in each of these areas if you were to embrace the Best Question Ever? In light of your past experience, current circumstances, and future hopes and dreams, what is the wise thing to do relationally? Morally? Spiritually?

Again, you don't have to act on your answers. Just take a moment to be painfully honest with yourself. What would you do differently in each of these areas if you were to evaluate each component of your life through the lens of the Best Question Ever?

Remember, you're not asking this question for anybody

but yourself. What's the wise thing *for me* to do? Resist the temptation to hide behind what others think or what is socially acceptable. What is the wise thing for you to do? You are a unique blend of past experiences, current circumstances, and future hopes and dreams. Wisdom allows you to customize the decision-making process to every area of your life. Don't miss this opportunity.

Think about how different your life would be now if you had been processing your options this way from the beginning. Imagine how different your life might look a year from now if you embrace the Best Question Ever from this point forward.

Okay, back to the real world. No need to feel guilty about what you just admitted to yourself but don't intend to do anything about. We've got several more chapters to wear down your resistance.

In the next section we are going to drill down a little further into a few of the areas we referred to throughout this section. Specifically, we are going to apply the Best Question Ever to the worlds of money, morality, and time.

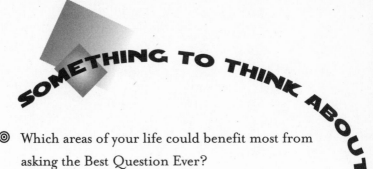

SOMETHING TO THINK ABOUT

◎ Which areas of your life could benefit most from asking the Best Question Ever?

◎ Why do you think it may be difficult to ask this question during important times in your life?

◎ If you don't ask this question while you're still young, what are some of the problems that you could face down the road?

◎ If you were to ask this question on a regular basis, how might you benefit?

◎ What is keeping you from asking yourself the Best Question Ever today?

PART II

A QUESTION OF TIME

TIME BANDITS
HAVING THE TIME
OF YOUR LIFE

Right now, it's easy to feel like you've got all the time in the world. I mean, there's a lot of life left to live. There's school, then probably marriage, kids, grandkids, etc. You've got a good fifty or sixty years to make up for any dumb mistakes you make in your teenage years, right? But what happens if bad choices during your teenage years continue to haunt you into your twenties and thirties and maybe even affect your future family or job?

You make choices every day about how to spend your time. *Should I call my friends or do my homework or watch that movie that's already five days overdue? Should I eat dinner with the family or hang out with my friends at the mall? Should I get up and spend time with God or grab a few more minutes of shut-eye?*

Almost every choice you make is influenced by a series of choices you've made prior to it. For example, if one day you wake up in your mid-thirties about fifty pounds over-weight, a chain smoker and jobless, it won't be the result of one or two decisions you made a few days before. It will be the cumulative result of decisions you began making in your teen years. Decisions made now and in the coming decade will someday come together as a picture of health (or sickness) and success (or failure) in your thirties. Don't believe me?

Think about the worst habit you have. Maybe it's overeating, maybe it's sleeping in, or maybe it's biting your fingernails. Can you think of the day when you started that bad habit? Did you wake up one morning and say, "I want to start a bad habit today"? Bad habits are developed over a period of time during which you make the same bad choices over and over again. Pretty soon, you begin making the choice without realizing you're making it. This is one reason it's important for you to be smart *now* about how you use your time. About how you use your words, your talents, and your energy.

It may seem like you've got all the time in the world to make changes, but the Bible assures us that our time here is limited. We only get so much of it. The book of Job puts it this way:

> Man's days are determined; you have decreed the
> number of his months and have set limits he cannot
> exceed. (Job 14:5, NIV)

Did you catch those last four words? "Limits he cannot exceed." You can overspend, overeat, and overachieve, but you can't "over-live."

The psalmist adds this insight regarding the relationship between our allotment of time and wisdom:

> Teach us to number our days aright, that we may gain
> a heart of wisdom. (Psalm 90:12, NIV)

I love that verse. Simply by recognizing that our days are limited, it says, we can come to understand just how important and valuable our time is.

WHICH WAY DID IT GO?

Sandra and I were married for almost five years before we had our first child. When we think back to those days of child-free living, we often wonder, *What in the world did we do with all that extra time?* Shouldn't we have something significant to show for those unencumbered years? Where did all that time go?

The answer: away. It went *away*.

And there's no way to recover a single minute of it.

That's the thing about time: You can't get it back. Once a second has passed, that second is gone forever. You can try and make up for lost time, but you will never be able to relive that exact moment. All the more reason to really think about what you do with your time.

Why do you spend time studying for tests and writing term papers instead of watching TV? Why do you practice for the big game instead of just showing up and using your "skills" to win? It's because you are looking ahead to a time and place where you want something good to happen. Something that will make you feel important, valued, and successful. Even now you have at least some vague ideas about the kinds of things you want to experience in the future. But are you using your time to point you in that direction?

In light of my past experiences, my current responsibilities, and my future hopes and dreams, what is the wisest way to invest my time?

Good question. The best, in fact. But how do you know which choice is the wise one? What *is* the wise thing to do with your time? Let's dig a little deeper.

CHIPPING AWAY

We're going to take a look at five pieces of a puzzle. A puzzle that includes important "pieces" of a principle that is true about time and how we use it. I call it a puzzle because if we don't put all of the pieces together, we don't get the entire picture. The first piece of this puzzle is this:

Small chunks of time invested = Bigger payoff down the road.

Working out is a good illustration of this. If you want to get in great shape and get those "six-pack" abs, it takes work. So one night you do your crunches and sit-ups. The next morning you look in the mirror, but there's no change! But you saw the commercial for "sixty-second abs," and you even pushed yourself to do *ninety* seconds. So what happened? Where's the results? I'm sure Brad Pitt got his abs in one sitting, right? Wrong. Rock-hard stomach muscles require consistent effort—small increments of time invested in crunches over a longer period of time.

The same is true if you're attempting to perfect your jump shot or learning to play an instrument. A little bit of concentrated effort several days a week over a period of six months will drastically improve your performance.

This principle is true for just about every facet of our lives, especially those pertaining to relationships. Let me list a few specific practices where consistency will make a difference: dinner with your family, time alone with God, church attendance, one-on-one time with your parents. No relationship worth having can be just a "one-stop shop" kind of thing. Relationships take time, and a little effort invested over a period of time, to make them all that God has planned for them to be.

So what's the benefit of eating dinner with your family instead of going out with your friends? In a couple of years, your family will still be there, but your "friends" might be ready to trade you in to hang out with a different crowd. Why is it important to spend time with God? Because the Creator of life wants to help you know how to live yours every day.

Can you think of any relationship that doesn't need time to make it stronger? Dating? Nope, needs time. Best friend? Still needs time. How about a dog? Try not spending time with your dog one week and see if you don't start getting the cold shoulder. So why should we wonder when our relationships with our parents and God are suffering? Check your calendar.

WHAT'S THE BIG DEAL?

This leads me to our second piece of the puzzle:

If we neglect the small chunks of time, we generally don't experience an immediate consequence.

Let's go back to the six-pack abs. You really want those abs, and you've even seen some results. But *American Idol* is on tonight and you can't miss that. Boy, that chocolate cake that Mom made for dessert looks pretty good. And you suddenly remember that you haven't called your best friend who reminded you fourteen times before you left school to call to catch up on the latest gossip. Oh, and you have a midterm tomorrow and you haven't even looked at the book. So much for those crunches.

So are your abs a lost cause? Has all of your hard work been in vain because of one night of neglect? Not really. In fact, you probably won't see any difference the next morning. Other than a mild upset stomach from the cake and some dark circles under the eyes from cramming late into the night.

This is true in most areas of life. If I don't study one night, no big deal. If I miss out on dinner with my family one evening, so what? If I forget to open my Bible one day, God will still be there tomorrow. It's deceiving but true that we rarely see any immediate consequences for neglecting one small bit of our lives. But if we keep doing this over and over, then we bump into our third point:

Neglect is like a snowball.

You can neglect your health for a week or two without any serious consequences. But strap that lifestyle on for ten or twelve years and the damage might be irreversible. Not because of a single night out or one particular meal. The effect is cumulative.

I know a student who recently graduated high school (barely) and went off to college. He wasn't able to get into the school of his choice, but he got in somewhere. His grades weren't quite what they needed to be in high school, and that didn't change much in college. He sure knew how to have fun, though. So when the final grades came, he was on his way back home.

Was he booted from school because he didn't study for one quiz or because he got a *D* on one paper? I don't think so. Over a period of time, his homework was put on a shelf and occasionally pulled down in a last-ditch attempt to squeak by. And in the end, this pattern of neglect snowballed into a one-way ticket home.

Neglect has a cumulative effect physically, relationally, spiritually, emotionally, and horticulturally. *Horticulturally?* I just looked out at my lawn. Neglect anything for a long period of time and you will have something to show for it. Usually a mess—a mess that can generate in us a wave of concern and even energy. Suddenly we realize what we have done and we rush out to the yard to reverse the consequences of our neglect.

But in the areas that matter most, a burst of energy and activity cannot reverse the consequences that accompany a season of neglect. More on that a little later.

IT DOESN'T ADD UP

The next stop in our five-point journey is something you have probably never thought about but have certainly experienced. While it is true that small, consistent investments of time add up to *good* things, and that consistent neglect adds up to *bad* things, the random pursuits that we allow to interrupt our important routines add up to *no-thing*:

Be careful not to let the things of no value get in the way of what is valuable.

Allow me to illustrate. Let's suppose that you were determined to improve your grades. You talked with your teachers, and they gave you specific steps to making this dream of yours a possibility. You knew what you needed to do and were determined to bring your *C* average up to a *B*. But along the road, a few things got in the way. You really can't even think of what they were, but they definitely did not include a textbook.

Now imagine that you have to sit down with your parents six months into the year and explain what you did instead of studying. How might that conversation go?

"What did you do instead of studying?" she asks.

"Um, I don't know. A lot of things, I guess."

"Well, let's think about it. Did you go to bed instead of studying?"

"Yeah, that's right. Sometimes I got a few extra hours of sleep."

"Okay, how many times?"

"I don't know."

"What else did you do instead of studying?"

"I saw some really good movies."

"How many?"

"I don't know."

"What did you do when you weren't watching movies?"

"Different stuff."

"What stuff?"

"I can't remember. Just stuff. Fun stuff."

"Okay. Did you listen in class?"

"Most of the time."

Here's the point: If you stack up all the stuff you did instead of studying, then added up their value, what would you end up with? Zero. The random pursuits that interrupt our important routines don't add up to *anything*. Well, actually, they add up to a lot of wasted time. There's never any cumulative value to all the things we do *instead of* the things we know are truly important.

What's the overall value of all the things a high school senior does instead of studying? Zero. What's the overall value of all the things a son does instead of spending time with his parents? Zero. What's the overall value of all the things that have interfered with your time with God? Zero.

When random activities constantly interfere with strategic deposits of time, it is like throwing away our most precious commodity. It is worse than wasting time—it's wasting your life.

This principle explains why we don't have more to show for our time. It all gets gobbled up with random, unquantifiable activities—activities that rob us of what's most important. When you add up all the what-I-did-instead-ofs, they always equal zero.

Before we dive into the fifth and final statement, let's take a look at what we have said so far.

1.   Small chunks of time invested = bigger payoff down the road.
2.   If we neglect the small chunks of time, we generally don't experience an immediate consequence.
3.   Neglect is like a snowball.
4.   Be careful not to let the things of no value get in the way of what is valuable.

If all of this is true and time equals life, what is the wise thing to do with your time?

LIVE AND LEARN
EDDIE MONEY WAS RIGHT

Ever hear of Eddie Money? Not Eddie Vedder. Eddie Money. Eddie was a big music star in the 1980s. Lots of hits. Very cool-looking guy. He usually appeared in still photos with a cigarette perched between his fingers. The reason I bring him up is that one of his biggest hits underscores the searing truth of our fifth and final statement about time. The song is "I Wanna Go Back." The chorus goes something like this:

> I know that things will never be the same.
> > I wanna go back
> and do it all over again,
> > but I can't go back, I know.

Eddie's right. We can't go back. We can't go back and relive, relove, retrieve, rearrange, reprioritize, redirect, or refocus. Looking back, there are times we want to go back. But we can't. You can't relive your childhood, your teens, or your twenties. You can't rewind that argument, replace that broken heart, or retrieve that lost purity.

Here's my fifth and final statement:

In the most important areas of your life, you cannot make up for lost time.

As students we could pull an all-nighter to make up for the studying we should have been doing all week. But in the world of relationships there are no all-nighters. You can't cram for a better relationship with your girlfriend or your spouse. Speeding up doesn't make up for lost time with your heavenly Father. The important areas of life require small deposits *all along the way*. And if you miss those opportunities, they are lost forever.

Let's take one final look at the pursuit of the six-pack abs. Time has gotten away from you. One day led to a week, which led to a month, which eventually led you down the path of "one-pack" abs instead. So what do you do? Is it possible to make up all that lost time in one night of sit-ups? Even if you could do a thousand sit-ups that night, the only thing you would end up with is a one-pack that's incredibly sore.

So what is the wise thing to do now?

Likewise, relationships are built on small, consistent

deposits of time. You can't cram for what's most important. If you want to connect with your family, you've got to be with them consistently, not randomly. A vacation or weekend getaway is a good way to commemorate or celebrate the past or even changes on the horizon. But neither can they compensate for consistent neglect.

So, once again, what is the wise thing for you to do?

REDEEMING THE TIME

With these five statements as a backdrop, look once again at Paul's warning to the believers in Ephesus:

> Therefore be careful how you walk, not as unwise men but as wise, *making the most of your time*, because the days are evil. (Ephesians 5:15–16, emphasis mine)

What in the world does Paul mean when he says, "Make the most of your time"? Paul is saying, "Get the full value out of your time—squeeze all the good you can out of every moment of your life." If you mess around with your time, you mess around with your life. Be wise. Make the most of your time. You can't go back and reinvest it. Your time is your life.

There are people who look at teenagers and think, *The only thing they know to do with time is waste it.* But I disagree. I don't believe Paul is speaking just to adults who have to know how to manage their time with family, friends, exercise, work. I believe his advice applies perfectly to your world of friends, school, family, dating, studying, fun, shopping... Shall I go on? Your time is split a dozen different ways, and God wants you to spend this time wisely. Take a step back and look at where your time is going.

If Job was right, and the number of our days really is determined, if there are limits we cannot exceed, then the issue of how we spend our time is of paramount importance. Indeed, time may be the most crucial arena in which to apply the Best Question Ever. So once again let me ask, in light of your past experience, your current circumstances, and your future hopes and dreams, how should you be allocating your time? What do you need to add to your schedule? What needs to be subtracted?

Your time is your life. What is the wise thing to do?

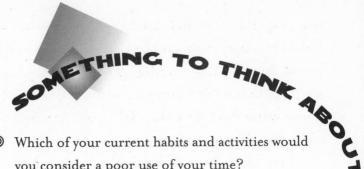

SOMETHING TO THINK ABOUT

◎ Which of your current habits and activities would you consider a poor use of your time?

◎ How could you potentially make better use of that time?

◎ What kinds of things do you do that you wouldn't consider either good or bad, but just a waste of time?

◎ What habits or activities are keeping you from making wise use of your time?

◎ Why is how you use your time so important?

PART III

A QUESTION OF MONEY

WORKING FOR THE BLING BLING
MANAGING YOUR DEAD PRESIDENTS

I can already hear the objections. *Money? Let Mom and Dad worry about money. I'm not making money—at least not enough to worry about.* Valid statement. Sure, you're at a stage of life where you probably don't have the pressure of managing money. But before we move on, let me ask you a few questions.

Ever have a job of any kind?

Do you have any possessions?

Are you ever planning on making money?

If you answered yes to any of these questions then you need to read this section. You might not be making a six-figure salary or have little mouths to feed, but you have *something* in your possession. Something that has been entrusted to you to use and take care of. Your 401(k) might be your Xbox, or your Mercedes might be Dad's old Lincoln. And one day, hopefully, you will be making money of your own. So why not get smart with your money now, even before you make it?

Everybody talks about money, about gettin' the bling bling. Look around. You've got superstar athletes willing to sacrifice their devotion to a team to pursue the almighty dollar. You've got contestants humiliating themselves on TV reality shows, trying to win millions. In the words of the modern-day poet 50 Cent, "Get rich or die tryin'."

Every time you turn on the TV or radio or open a magazine, you're hit with the message:

More Money = More Stuff = A Better Life

But how true is this, really?

The truth is, if more people thought about money and possessions through the lens of the Best Question Ever, they might spend their money differently. Some people would drive a different car, live in a smaller house, or maybe shop at Target instead of Abercrombie. It doesn't matter what you've got; what matters is what you do with it. And that's usually where we mess up.

Believe it or not, how you treat money when you get out of school and get a job will be the direct result of how you treat it now. If you have $20 and you can't wait to spend that entire $20, then one day when you make $20,000 you'll find you can't wait to spend $20,000. It becomes a never-ending cycle of always looking for and wanting *more*.

Unless you learn how to manage your money.

Learn how to control it before it controls you.

Money is a part of our everyday lives. There's no getting around that. We don't trade cows anymore to buy food. If we need or want to buy anything it takes money. This information is not new to God, but His perspective on how to deal with our money is new to most of the general public.

In fact, God wants us to be rich!

But first we need to learn *His* definition of "rich."

RICH REDEFINED

Do you have clothes? Did you eat today? Do you or your parents have a car? By the standards of a large part of the rest of the world, you would be considered pretty wealthy. In fact, millions of people all over the world would love to be in your shoes right now.

So how does it feel to be rich and envied?

You probably have no idea, and here's why.

There is a big difference between *being* rich and *feeling* rich. We don't feel rich because we are always comparing our possessions to what everyone else has. John's got the nicer car. Sharon's house has a hot tub. Jill's family visited the White House instead of Grandma's house for summer vacation. So how can you consider yourself rich? Those are the "rich" people, right?

I beg to differ.

The rich man is the one who realizes that everything he has was given to him by God and that God wants him to use these resources wisely. Who is more rich, the man who inherits $100,000 dollars and buys a $100,000 Ferrari, or the man who inherits $50,000 and buys a $10,000 Hyundai Sonata? Most of us would say the first guy because he is riding in style. But what is he going to wear while riding in that fine set of wheels? And who's going to pay for his gas?

You see, the guy who inherited $50,000 has money left over; he is using his inheritance wisely. When we use wisdom in dealing with our money and possessions, we are indeed rich.

ASKING THE WRONG QUESTIONS

Of all the areas of life that require wisdom, this one should be the easiest to get a handle on. Making decisions about time, relationships, and even morality requires us to consider such intangibles as passion, fear, and God's calling. But money is simple: A certain amount comes in and you tell it what to do. That's pretty much it.

The fact is, in this country, most money problems stem from poor financial management, not low income. How do we know this? Because the two biggest crises Americans face today are obesity and consumer debt. We eat too much and we spend too much. Neither of these problems is caused by earning too little.

But as usual, our propensity is to look for someone else to blame. So overweight people blame McDonald's, while financially overextended people blame the economy or the president or their employers.

So what's happening? Why is it so easy for us to abandon common sense when it comes to our money? Why do we spend so foolishly? Why do we intentionally take on the unnecessary pressure that comes with credit card debt and then complain about it?

Is it greed? Maybe. Is it stupidity? Probably not. Are we all just consumed with keeping up with the people around us? I'm sure that's part of it. But I think there's something else that keeps us on the financial treadmill. We have allowed culture to influence the way we manage money by teaching us to ask all the wrong questions.

Can I afford it?

What will the monthly payment be?

How much can I borrow?

Is it on sale?

The assumption is that if I *can* make it work financially, I *should* make it work. If I *can* afford it, I *should* afford it. If I *can* borrow it, I *should* borrow it.

The reason we so easily get upside-down financially is because everybody who has anything to sell is working overtime to move us in that direction. The only person looking out for your best interest financially is—you guessed it—*you*! And that means you must ask yourself a *different* set of questions.

The conventional questions are fine for conventional people, but you don't want to be a conventional person, do you? If you look *conventional* up in the thesaurus you will find these synonyms: *standard, normal, typical*.

Think about it. Do you want to be a standard person? How about normal? Typical? Conventional is what everybody else is doing. And you remember what your mom has always said about that: "If everybody jumped off a cliff, would you jump, too?"

COULD VERSUS SHOULD

Conventional financial wisdom is built on the premise that if you can, you should. But when you begin to evaluate your financial decisions through the lens of the Best Question Ever, all of that changes. You will stop asking, "What *can* I do?" and ask, "What *should* I do?" Instead of, *"Can* I afford it?" you will ask, *"Should* I afford it?"

In light of your current financial picture and your future financial hopes and dreams, what is the wise thing to do?

The Best Question Ever frees you from the conventional approach to finances—an approach that has robbed most American adults of the freedom that could be theirs if they

would simply live on what they make instead of what they can borrow. The Best Question Ever allows you to be content with more of what you have and less of what you want.

UNCONVENTIONAL WISDOM
LIVING LIKE A KING
(OR QUEEN)

In what has come to be known as the Sermon on the Mount, Jesus described how people with perfect faith would respond to life. We read it and frown. His expectations seem so unrealistic, so impractical. But if you really believe God is who He says He is and that He will do what He has promised to do, then Jesus' words make perfect sense.

His words regarding our endless pursuit of *stuff* are particularly challenging. But if taken to heart they have the potential to completely reorder your thinking about the pursuit of wealth. I imagine you have read these verses before, but take a moment to read them again. Don't rush. Allow these words to sink in.

> "Therefore I tell you, do not worry about your life, what you will eat or drink; or about your body, what you will wear. Is not life more important than food, and the body more important than clothes? Look at the birds of the air; they do not sow or reap or store away in barns, and yet your heavenly Father feeds them. Are you not much more valuable than they? Who of you by worrying can add a single hour to his life?
>
> "And why do you worry about clothes? See how the lilies of the field grow. They do not labor or spin. Yet I tell you that not even Solomon in all his splendor was dressed like one of these. If that is how God clothes the grass of the field, which is here today and tomorrow is thrown into the fire, will he not much more clothe you, O you of little faith? So do not worry, saying, 'What shall we eat?' or 'What shall we drink?' or 'What shall we wear?' For the pagans run after all these things, and your heavenly Father knows that you need them. But seek first his kingdom and his righteousness, and all these things will be given to you as well." (Matthew 6:25–33, NIV)

God wants to take care of our needs. He is more concerned about our needs than we are. Our problem is that we generally confuse our "wants" with our "needs." If we want something enough, we will soon convince ourselves that it is, in fact, a need. That's when we begin making dumb mistakes with our money.

Jesus makes an interesting statement here that gives us the inside scoop on living rich. He says, "Seek first *His* Kingdom." Did you get that? His kingdom, not our kingdom. The complete opposite of what most of us do as we surround ourselves with creature comforts.

But Jesus makes us a promise: Seek His kingdom first "and all these things will be given to you as well." "All these things" is the stuff of life that we pursue to the neglect of God's kingdom. "All these things" is what we eat, where we live, what we wear. It is the stuff that consumes the majority of our financial resources.

Essentially, Jesus is offering us a deal. He will take responsibility for our needs if we will make His kingdom our priority. If we will transfer our concerns to pursue what's important to Him, He will take responsibility for what is important to us. This is why I can say with confidence that seeking Him first with our money is how we can ensure His intervention and provision in that area of our lives.

REORDERING YOUR FINANCIAL PRIORITIES

As you look at what you have now, and as you prepare for your financial future, I want to talk about five things to do with your money in order of their importance. Odds are you won't hear this many other places. In fact, most people reverse the order. But I strongly believe that by exercising wisdom and honoring God with your money, you will experience God's best for you in this area of your life. Here's the list:

1. Give it.
2. Save it.
3. Pay taxes.
4. Repay debt.
5. Spend it.

GIVE FIRST

If giving to kingdom work invites God into your finances, then the first check you ought to write after you get paid is a check to support His kingdom. This is how you "seek first" with your money. When you give first it is the equivalent of saying, "Father, I want to make sure Your kingdom is fully funded. I'll live on the leftovers."

Give before you spend. How much? The New Testament doesn't give us a percentage. But I can't imagine giving anything less than a tithe—that is, 10 percent. It's a small price to pay to bring God into the mix. Besides, it's all His anyway. If you don't have enough faith to begin with a tithe, then pick a lower percentage. But make sure you choose a percentage. Percentage giving is the way to begin.

Teens often respond to this by saying, "How can I give

away what I barely have any of myself? Besides, if I only make twenty bucks this week, is God really going to miss my two-dollar tithe?" They are missing the point. God doesn't need our money, but we need His perspective. Giving a tithe may be more beneficial for the giver than for anyone else. It is another step in understanding God's view of what it means to be rich. So start giving now, no matter how much you have. Set a pattern that you will follow when you're older, and you will never regret it.

Pay Yourself Second

What's the wise thing to do once you have funded God's kingdom? Fund your own. Remember, there is a difference between a want and a need. You need food, but you want a new CD. Is it wrong to buy the CD? Not necessarily, but it can be if you trade in your food money for your listening pleasure. The goal here is to take care of the "have to's" and still save some along the way. Someday soon you will be paying for bills, groceries, clothes, cars, etc. Start now by wisely looking at the money you have and separating the needs from the wants.

Retire Debt

Hopefully, you don't have any debt yet. But if they haven't already, someone soon will be offering to give you a credit card. Or two. Or three. And if you're considering going to college, you will be hit hard with the possibility of going deep into debt.

What is debt? It's simply owing somebody else. You'll have many opportunities in life to "pay for it later." Some people call it the magic of plastic. The problem is, most people enjoy the magic a little too much and they end up owing huge sums of money down the road. Money they don't have.

It's a good rule of thumb to avoid debt—no matter how appealing those credit card offers sound.

Pay Your Taxes

Again, this is something you may not be dealing with yet, but taxes are a fact of life. Yet if you give generously and save wisely, you will pay less in taxes.

Spend

Finally, we get to the item that generally tops the list for most of us. Once you have given, saved, paid down debt, and funded your local, state, and national governments, you get to go shopping!

"With what?" you may ask.

With the leftovers.

Now before you decide to line your birdcage with pages from this book, I want you to think about something: What if you were to prioritize in this manner, starting with your first job? Think of how much money you could save. Think of the extra cash you could have if you never have to juggle credit card bills. This isn't the *easy* thing to do, but I would argue that it is the *wise* thing to do.

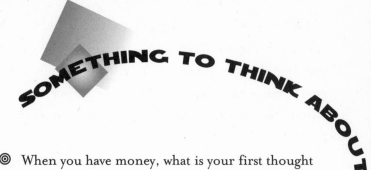

SOMETHING TO THINK ABOUT

◎ When you have money, what is your first thought on how to spend it? On yourself? On others? On God's work?

◎ Why is it important to be wise with your money?

◎ Do you tend to have a hard time being wise with your money? Why?

◎ Does God need your money? If not, why do you suppose He is so concerned with how you use it?

◎ If God owns everything, including money, how does that change how you should use money?

PART IV

A QUESTION OF MORALITY

SEX FOR DUMMIES
WHY AREN'T THESE
PEOPLE SMILING?

If you're like me, at about this part of a book, you start skimming—looking over parts of sentences without actually reading. Let me encourage you, *please do not do this!* Over the next few pages, we're going to be looking at an area in which I believe the Best Question Ever means the most in the lives of teenagers: morality. Meaning dating, sex, your thought life, etc. So stick with me here. I would hate for you to miss this incredibly important topic. And besides, we're talking about sex.

The simple message of these next few chapters is one I have spent fifteen years of my life trying to instill in the minds and hearts of American teenagers. Some listened and applied it. Through the years I have received countless letters and e-mails from students thanking me for this uncomplicated yet profound principle. Many of these former students are married now and enjoying the rewards of having chosen the path of wisdom in this area of life.

Unfortunately, many chose to not listen. And that's understandable. Every day, teenagers are bombarded with messages and images that support a different viewpoint—a view fueled by the God-given passions raging inside their overstimulated and underdisciplined bodies. Besides, I'm old enough to be their dad. What could *I* possibly know?

Nothing has stolen more dreams, dashed more hopes, broken up more families, and messed up more people psychologically than our propensity to disregard God's commands regarding sexual purity. Most of the major social ills in America are caused by, or fueled by, the misuse of our sexuality. If issues related to sexual impurity—teen pregnancy, addiction to pornography, AIDS and other sexually transmitted diseases, abortion, the psychological effects associated with abortion, sexual abuse, incest, rape, and all sexual addictions—were to suddenly disappear from society, imagine the resources we would have available to apply to the handful of issues that would remain.

Since God gives us choices in life, there will always be those who choose to walk down the path of sexual impurity. This, too, is a fact of life. But for the sake of those who are willing to listen, the warning must be sounded.

Slow Learners

I started this book by saying that we have all done things we regret. We regret some decisions because they are embarrassing. Other regrets stem from decisions that ate up our time or wasted our resources. But no regret runs deeper than the regret associated with unwise moral decisions. In time you may find you are able to laugh about wasted money and poor time management. But when it comes to moral failure, time doesn't help. Nobody laughs about a teen pregnancy, AIDS, or the loss of one's purity. In the arena of moral failure, the regret runs deep and the pain can traverse generations. Chances are, your greatest regrets in life fall somewhere within this category.

The strange thing is, as predictable as the outcomes are, we humans don't appear to have learned very much. One would think that after losing thousands of people to sexually transmitted diseases and watching a generation or two of kids grow up without fathers in their homes, we might have learned something. But alas, lust and greed continue to drive us past the limits afforded by common sense.

I was reminded of how predictable the outcomes are one day when a youth leader and a teenage girl from her group came up to me, crying. I thought someone was hurt and was about to go and find the first-aid kit. The leader stopped me and asked if they could talk. I said, "Sure. What about?"

"Him!" the girl said. I could tell from the way she said it that she wasn't talking about God.

"Who?" I asked.

She proceeded to tell me about her ex-boyfriend. Ex- by only a few days, which explained the emotional onslaught I was witnessing.

"What happened?"

"It all started at this party we were at. I had told him for a long time that I wasn't ready to have sex with him, but he kept pressuring me. I had seen him flirting with other girls, and I was afraid of losing him."

Uh, oh. I knew where this was going.

"I wanted to show him how much I loved him, so I gave in. He was the first guy I ever slept with. But as it turns out, I was not his first."

"How did you know?"

"He told me later that I might need to go to the doctor and get checked out. That he might have passed something on to me. What do I do?"

The amazing thing was that this was a girl who knew better. She had heard time and again of the consequences of premarital sexual intercourse. But she thought her situation was different.

She found out the hard way that it wasn't.

WHEN THE FOG ROLLS IN

Do you know why many young people today make foolish decisions when it comes to sex and morality? It's because they think that *their* situation is unique—that they are going through something that nobody else would understand. That they have an unusual capacity for overcoming any obstacle that might stand between them and their hormones.

"But you don't understand! He really loves me."

"There's nothing wrong with having the Internet."

"Fooling around isn't sex."

As long as you are convinced that your situation and feelings are unique, you will resist the Best Question Ever. Now, that might seem to contradict the entire premise of the question—after all, your uniqueness is what makes this question so powerful. But in this context we are not talking about your individuality as it relates to your past, your present, and your future dreams. In that way, you *are* unique.

But there is nothing unique about your circumstances, your emotions, your desires, and your passions. And as long as you deceive yourself into thinking that you are the first to feel what you are feeling, you will chase those feelings away and forget about making the wise choice. And at the end of the day you will discover that you are not so unique after all. The outcomes are predictable. Lonely is lonely, no matter how popular you are. Addicted is addicted, no matter who you know. Guilty is guilty, no matter what you drive. Depressed is depressed, no matter what pill you take.

What's your story? What circumstances have brought you to where you are right now? What is the wise thing for you to do?

Brace yourself before you ask this question.

That road can get very bumpy.

HINDSIGHT
THE STORY OF
CLAY AND BETH

Think for a moment about your greatest moral regret. Think about that one event that you felt really bad about afterward. That night at the party. That glance at the computer screen. That kiss. That night in his car.

I told you this might get a bit bumpy.

I know, it is probably something you work hard not to think about. You may have promised yourself you would never think about it again. And that may have been a good idea. But now that I've dredged it up, hold on to it for just a moment. There may even be a whole list for you to choose from. And they may not be in the distant past. Whatever the case, play along and pick one.

Now think back to the decisions that led up to that one regret. The choices you made beforehand that got you to the place you wish you could take back.

I wish I had never gone out with him.

I wish I had never called her.

I wish I had never accepted his invitation.

I wish I had never hit "Enter."

I wish I had listened to my mom.

If you think back far enough, you can probably string together a series of decisions that led you to the brink of the moment or season you now regret.

My point?

Our greatest moral regrets are always preceded by a *series* of unwise choices. Not wrong choices, not impermissible, not illegal, but unwise. We walk ourselves right up to the edge of disaster by making choices that aren't necessarily "wrong." So we don't hesitate. We jump in. Then we defend our actions with the anemic excuse, "I couldn't help myself," followed by the equally ridiculous question, "How did I get into this mess?"

A more helpful and honest question to ask is, "How did I get *myself* into this mess?" The answer to that question is the same for everybody. *Everybody.* Once we follow our desires, there ain't nothing new under the sun.

How did we get ourselves into such a mess? We made a series of unwise choices. Unwise choices that sent us beyond the point of no return. The names and faces change, but the sequences and outcomes are tragically similar. We may think our situation is different and, therefore, what is wise for most isn't wise for us.

But in the end...well, I think we've covered that sufficiently.

You know what's so ironic? When someone we know begins inching toward moral disaster, we can see it so clearly. Take Clay and Beth, for example.

STUDY SESSION

Clay and Beth sit next to each other every day in biology class. Clay is pretty cool and a nice guy, and Beth enjoys talking with him during those boring lectures (which happen more often than not). Beth is a good moral girl who wants to date the right guy and is even strongly considering "saving herself" for marriage. She thinks Clay is kind of cute, but probably not her type.

One day, Clay and Beth are assigned to work together on a project. This project will take a lot of after-school time to finish, so Clay thinks of asking Beth over for a "study session." Beth is not sure what to think, since she doesn't know much about Clay and has never been to a guy's house to study. But how else could they get the assignment done? Beth agrees to come over on Wednesday night at eight.

Clay tells her their basement is finished, so they won't be

disturbed by his parents or his sister. Clay gives his address to Beth and says, "See you at eight?"

Beth nods.

So far, nobody has done anything wrong. In fact, you may have found yourself in a similar situation at some point. But before we go on in the story, let's ask ourselves a few questions. Is there anywhere else they could meet to study? Does it have to be just the two of them? What does it matter if they study in the basement or the kitchen? Hmm. Let's return to their story.

A few weeks later, Clay tells Beth that he really enjoyed studying with her and that she makes it very easy for him to express his "lack of understanding" in biology class. She feels a little warmth inside as Clay begins to open up to her and share. *Wow, this guy is pretty sincere. Maybe he isn't so bad after all.* She smiles and says, "Me, too."

As the semester wears on, Clay and Beth begin to spend more and more time together. Studying together, occasionally even meeting at the local Starbucks to catch a quick latte after school. People begin to wonder and speculate that they're a couple. Some of the speculation turns to gossip, but there's nothing they can do about that.

One night, Clay's parents go out of town. He had originally planned to hold a big party at his house, but he cancels it so he can have Beth over for a movie night.

So where am I going with this? You may be reading and wondering, *They sound like a cute couple. I wouldn't mind having a rela-*

tionship like that. They haven't done anything wrong. This is true. They've done nothing immoral or wrong. Yet.

LATER THAT NIGHT...

Beth doesn't tell her parents that Clay's folks are out of town. They wouldn't understand. Knowing her dad, his answer would be a definite, "Are you crazy?!" So she asks her parents to drop her off, all the while making them believe that Clay's parents are home.

What's the difference? Beth thinks. *Other than that we can cuddle without the weirdness of having Clay's mom and dad in the next room.*

Clay welcomes Beth at the door with an "I'm glad it's just the two of us tonight." Beth nods and they settle on the couch to watch the movie.

How romantic. It's obvious that Clay and Beth have just moved on to another stage of their relationship. It's the "just the two of us" stage. Once again, we need to stop and ask ourselves if there is anything wrong going on here. Has anyone gone too far sexually? Has there been any inappropriate physical contact? Nope. But they have taken a step closer to the edge—an edge they could step over at any moment and fall to the point of no return. The place where all rational thinking goes out the window. Where hormones and emotions collide, resulting in a moment that nobody was ready for.

I believe we can stop right here with this story. You probably know the rest of the story, as well as the rest of the relationship. Because we all know how close that edge is and that it doesn't take much to plunge over it. It's an edge that, if we would only ask the Best Question Ever, would grow smaller and smaller in our rearview mirror.

LIFE RULES
LIVING FAR FROM THE EDGE

The edge is a place we like to live. It's a place of adventure and living dangerously. In rock climbing this is exciting. But when it comes to morality it is foolish. I have talked with hundreds of teenagers who had set up boundaries, determined not to have sex before marriage. Like Beth, they had high moral standards and had committed themselves to waiting. For many of them, however, "no sex before marriage" was their only boundary. They had determined that they were not going to "do it," but had done nothing else. I'm sad to say that many of these students didn't accomplish their goal.

Why is that? Why did they fail when they had determined so strongly in their minds that sex before marriage was wrong. It was because they were willing to live right up on the edge, and eventually, the wind blew too strongly or they simply slipped. When it comes to morality and sexual purity, we cannot live on the edge if we hope to be successful. In fact, our boundaries need to be drawn far away from the edge so that if we do slip, we've got some ground to regain our balance on before we tumble over the edge.

PLAYING IT SAFE

The Best Question Ever will lead you away from the brink of a decision you may regret to a place of safety. This fact alone is why it is so easy to disregard the Best Question Ever in the arena of sexuality. Like you, I don't want to miss out on anything life has to offer. So my natural inclination is to ask, "Where's the line between right and wrong?" Once that is established, I want to cozy up to the line and live right there. To do otherwise may mean missing out on something good.

At the same time, I don't want to do anything now that will haunt me in the future. And there's a part of me that wants to please my heavenly Father. So once I've recognized where the line is, I try not to cross it. The problem with this approach is that there is no margin for error. In most areas of life that is not a problem. If the speed limit is fifty-five miles per hour, I drive fifty-five miles per hour. If my thoughts drift and I find myself roaring down the highway at sixty miles per hour, no harm done. I just ease off the gas. When I was sixteen and my curfew was midnight, I tried to time it so that I arrived home right at midnight. I gave myself no margin for error. If I was a few minutes late, no problem, no consequences. If you violate the guidelines of your diet for a day, no problem. You just ease back into your routine the following day.

But when you cross certain lines sexually, there are *always* consequences, sometimes for the rest of your life. Slipping over this line can result in raising a child that you were not prepared—emotionally, physically, or financially—to take care of. Or it can result in unneeded and unwanted comparisons with your future spouse. For many young men, it means living with the constant distraction of images they can't erase from their minds. It means young ladies losing the opportunity to give themselves wholly to their husbands on their wedding night. It can mean living with the burden of an incurable disease. As in the case of three friends of mine, crossing certain lines sexually can mean death—death that leaves a hole in a family, a mother mourning the loss of a child, brothers and sisters devastated. In the case of the HIV epidemic in Africa, crossing certain lines morally has resulted in hundreds of thousands of homeless children.

Let me be blunt. To leave yourself no margin for error morally is about the most insensitive thing you can do to those you love. Relationally, it is a death wish. It is the worst kind of arrogance. It is tantamount to a recovering alcoholic walking into a bar and sitting down on a bar stool, all the while justifying his actions with the excuse, "There's nothing wrong with being here as long as I'm not drinking."

It's one thing to know this. It's another to know how to do it.

WHAT WAS GOD THINKING?

In the Bible, God doesn't have a whole lot to say about dating. Why is that? If sex and dating is such a big deal, why didn't God say something about it? Well, if you were living in ancient Judea, odds are you would be married by now. Teenagers were married and raising families. In our culture today we're not getting married until later in life. So does this mean God's plan for sex has changed? Not one bit. God never changes His laws because of what is socially, culturally, or politically acceptable.

So this seems like a mean trick, huh? You may be sixteen and looking at a good eight years at least before you even *think* about marriage. In fact, your hormones have been raging for some four or five years now. How can God expect you to survive this? Why would He place within you a desire that cannot be fulfilled for many years to come?

God never promised us that everything in life would be easy. In fact, most of the things in life that fulfill us, we have to wait for. We have to wait until we are emotionally and physically prepared to handle it. God knows when that is, and His plan is the only thing that will ever fulfill us 100 percent.

So how do we do it? If we must wait in this world of indulgence, how can we hope to survive? How can we live far enough from the edge so that we can endure the temptations that come our way? Let's take a look at what Paul wrote to the church in Corinth, a place that can best be described as "sex crazed." This is what he said about temptation:

No temptation has seized you except what is common to man. And God is faithful; he will not let you be tempted beyond what you can bear. But when you are tempted, he will also provide a way out so that you can stand up under it. (1 Corinthians 10:13, NIV)

How is this supposed to help us? Things make more sense if we break down the verse into three parts.

EVERYBODY'S DOING IT!

No temptation has seized you except what is common to man...

Let me clear this up for you. First of all, everybody is *not* doing it. But everyone *is* tempted by it. Sexual temptation is everywhere. Open up a magazine, watch a commercial, look at a billboard, watch a movie—sex is everywhere. Why do you think there's a sex scene that makes no sense in the plot of a movie? Because "sex sells." Advertisers hope that while you're paying attention to the sexual elements in their commercials then maybe you'll associate pleasure with the product they're trying to sell you.

From the very beginning, temptation has been a part of our lives. Sexual temptation is nothing new, nor is it something that only you struggle with. But you *are* unique in how and when you are tempted. So be honest with yourself. Don't kid yourself into thinking that you are bigger than the temptation. Identify and avoid situations in which you know you are tempted to think or act on your urges.

I Can Handle It

And God is faithful; He will not let you be tempted beyond what you can bear...

"But I couldn't help it."

"It just happened."

I've heard these excuses a hundred times, and I cringe every time I hear them because I know that the person saying it has fallen for a lie. One of the oldest lies around. The lie that says, "I can't help it—it's just who I am." Yes, God created us to enjoy sex, but at the right time and in the proper context: marriage.

Let me give you a word of advice. If you allow a battle to happen between your will and your hormones, you're in trouble. Odds are, your hormones will win. I would be willing to bet money on it. God never intended for your will to completely protect you in this area. He gave us something called "wisdom" to guide us here. God would never place something so powerful in you and then leave you all alone. He will never allow you to go through more than you can handle. The problem happens when you don't look for the way out.

WHEN THE DOOR IS CRACKED

But when you are tempted, He will also provide a way out so that you can stand up under it.

Let me ask you a question. Would you rather have to find an exit while standing in the middle of a burning building, or be standing next to the exit in a burning building? Obviously a no-brainer. Who would want to have to search for the exit from the middle of a smoke-filled building that is about to burn to the ground? First of all, it's difficult to find the door; and second, you might not make it out alive.

But when it comes to looking for the way out morally, we often find ourselves deep in the heart of a burning building. We may wish that we could get out, but the heat and the smoke make it next to impossible. Maybe we should have looked for the way out a little sooner. Maybe right before we walked in the front door.

You see, the way out could have been when your dad told you not to go out with this guy, or when your parents told you that you shouldn't have Internet access in your room. God will always provide a way of escape, but that escape becomes more difficult the closer we get to the edge.

This is why the Best Question Ever is so helpful. When it comes to sexual temptation, we tend to wait until it's way too late before we look for the way of escape. When first faced with a potentially tempting situation, we need to ask ourselves the question, *In light of past experiences, my present circumstance, and my future hopes and dreams, what is the wise thing to do in this relationship? What is the wise thing to do in this situation? And where is the way of escape?*

There can be different exits for different situations, but we have to be honest with ourselves as to when is the right time to "get the heck out of Dodge!"

FLEE!
The Wisdom of Flight

As it turns out, Paul wasn't finished addressing the church in Corinth regarding this issue of resisting temptation:

> Regarding sexual immorality, pursue all manner of sensuality and impurity, yet remain faithful to God and your spouse. Men, gaze upon women in a lustful fashion until your heart is full, but do not touch that which is forbidden. Women, dress in a manner that provokes the lustful passions of the men around you, but in your actions remain faithful to your husband.

That's from 3 Corinthians, the lost epistle.

Just kidding. Go ahead and look—it's not in there. But doesn't that pretty much describe our society's approach?

Actually, what Paul told them was much simpler: "Flee from sexual immorality" (1 Corinthians 6:18, NIV).

The Greek term translated here as *flee* means "flee." As in, "run really fast in the opposite direction." No doubt you have fled from something in your lifetime—an oncoming car, your neighbor's dog, a linebacker, your big sister. We all know what it means to flee.

When I was in third grade, I shot my sister with a toy arrow. My dad took the arrow and began chasing me through the house. I fled. I ran into the bathroom and sat down on the toilet to keep him from spanking me with the arrow. Unfortunately, the lid was open and I fell in wearing my favorite footy pajamas. My dad laughed so hard that he couldn't spank me.

When I was in fifth grade, I was walking with a buddy across a pasture when we looked up and saw a herd of cattle stampeding in our direction. We fled. When we reached the barbed-wire fence, we dove underneath and rolled to safety.

There is a certain emotion associated with fleeing. Fear. We flee when we know we are in danger. Fear prompts us to flee. The reason we don't flee sexual immorality is that we don't fear it; we naively believe we can handle it. So instead of fleeing, we flirt with it. We snuggle up next to it. We dance around the edges. After all, we aren't doing anything *wrong*.

There's nothing wrong with standing out in the middle

of an open pasture with a herd of stampeding cattle heading your way, either. There's not one verse of Scripture that prohibits such behavior. I have never heard a sermon on the subject. In fact, the United States Constitution protects your right to do so. But nonetheless, it is a stupid thing to do. And by the time you've learned your lesson, you won't have another opportunity to apply what you've learned.

IN A CATEGORY ALL ITS OWN

Paul doesn't stop with his four-word warning. He goes on to make one of the most profound statements in the New Testament: "All other sins a man commits are outside his body, but he who sins sexually sins against his own body."

Sexual sin is in a category all its own. It is the most dangerous kind of sin. Anyone who has done any significant amount of counseling knows this to be the case. Sexual sin wreaks havoc with the soul, whether male or female. It has the potential to wreak havoc on our physical bodies as well. The shame runs deep and the regret runs wide, often seeping into every facet of a person's life. Long after men and women come to grips with God's forgiveness, those who have sinned sexually still wrestle to forgive *themselves*. I don't know why I bother to write this in the third person. We all know this to be true from personal experience, either our own or that of someone close to us.

So flee! Don't hesitate. Don't look back. Don't try to

endure it. Don't flirt with it. Don't fool yourself. Don't try to be strong. Run! Like a coiled snake, sexual temptation has a considerable striking distance. You are never as safe as you think.

FLEEING 101

In light of your past experience, current circumstances, and future hopes and dreams, what is the wise thing for you to do in order to avoid regret in this area of life?

If your past is tarnished with moral failure, then you have to consider your history to protect your future. Your past points to the fact that you are more susceptible in this area than the average person; consequently, you can't be content with average boundaries.

Through the years, I have had numerous conversations with young men who have been very sexually active before coming to faith in Christ. From their past experience, dating was almost synonymous with sex—sex was pretty much the goal of a date. Coming to faith in Christ didn't automatically erase those leanings.

My advice to a young man or woman coming from that kind of past is always the same: Don't date for a year. I tell them to get out their calendars, look ahead one year, and circle the date. They always stare at me with the same look of disbelief. Some listen, some don't. Those who do come back and thank me. Those who don't, don't.

Why a year? Isn't that a bit extreme? Yep. But those who've taken the challenge will tell you that what God did in their hearts during that year prepared them to venture back into the world of romance with a completely different perspective on relationships. Many of these young men and women are happily married now. They consider their decision not to date to be a defining moment in their lives.

I know young ladies who have written off dating until after they graduate high school. I know teenagers who refuse to go out with anyone unless it is on a group date. I know young men who have canceled their Internet service. These are people who, because of their past, took extreme measures in response to the Best Question Ever. And while their friends chuckled, they were set free.

You Must Decide

As we said earlier, the Best Question Ever enables us to plan *not* to get into trouble. Asking the question enables us to stand our ground against the seemingly overwhelming current of culture. Applied to the arena of sexual purity, the Best Question Ever enables us to make a clean break with the past and move purposely toward our hopes and dreams.

But to leverage this powerful principle you will need to pre-decide some things. You need to pre-decide about what are and are not appropriate places to be. You need to pre-decide the type of person you need to date, and do not compromise. You need to pre-decide your entertainment options, the music you listen to and the movies you watch.

All of this might strike you as a bit overboard. Extreme. Maybe even legalistic. But here's what I know. When teenagers are confronted with the consequences of their moral impropriety, they all say the same thing: "I would give anything—*anything*—to be able to go back and undo what I've done."

Anything? Isn't that a bit extreme? They don't think so. Perhaps you, too, would be willing to go to extreme measures if it meant being able to undo certain moments of your life. So why not take extreme precautions up front instead of facing the reality that even extreme sacrifices on the back end won't erase the past?

If you don't decide some of these things ahead of time, somebody else will decide for you. If you don't have your own personal standards, somebody else will force theirs on you. Everyone agrees that there are lines that shouldn't be crossed. You must conduct your relationships within the boundaries you have set for yourself in light of your past experience, your current circumstances, and your future hopes and dreams.

Had you adopted the Best Question Ever a few years ago, perhaps your greatest regrets could have been avoided. If you adopt it now, future regrets can be avoided. The Best Question Ever enables you to experience what God originally intended when He gave mankind the precious gift of sexuality.

A DESIGNER GIFT

In the beginning, God didn't just create the heavens and the earth. In the beginning, God created sex. It was His idea! Is God good, or what? Better yet, after creating it, He gave it to us as a gift! Let's all stop and give God a huge round of applause!

He gave sex to us as a gift—a gift that comes with instructions. Contrary to popular opinion, the guidelines for using this Designer gift were created to enhance our experience, not diminish it. God is not against sex. He's all for it! The parameters He has set are evidence that He is for *you* as well. For within these boundaries a man and a woman are able to experience something that goes way beyond physical satisfaction. When sex is enjoyed the way God originally intended, the result is intimacy, not just pleasure. When we ignore God's guidelines, we pay the price in the very realm sex was designed to enhance—intimacy.

So once again we find ourselves asking this confining yet liberating question: What is the wise thing to do?

In light of my past experience, what is the wise thing to do going forward? In light of what's going on in my life right now—my physical, emotional, and spiritual health—what is the wise thing to do? And as I contemplate the future—an intimate sexual relationship with my spouse—what is the wise thing to do?

No, it won't always be easy to do the wise thing. But you've already experienced enough of life to know that it will be worth it.

SOMETHING TO THINK ABOUT

◎ What causes you to struggle when it comes to the area of sexual temptation?

◎ Why is it important that you ask the Best Question Ever when it comes to sex?

◎ Would you say that the majority of your friends are wise when it comes to sex? Why or why not?

◎ Why is God concerned about sexual temptation in your life?

◎ If you asked the Best Question Ever when faced with temptation, what would change about your moral life?

PART V

WISDOM FOR THE ASKING

HIDE AND SEEK
WHAT TO DO WHEN YOU
DON'T KNOW WHAT TO DO

It's time to head down the home-stretch here. As we have seen, asking the Best Question Ever in the important areas of our lives will be life changing. By asking, "What is the wise thing to do?" we will usually be able to determine which way to go, which decision to make. But what about when we still feel like we're in a fog? When either choice could possibly be the wise choice?

Sure, the Best Question Ever will reduce your options, but it might not necessarily single out *one*. What should you do if you are genuinely committed to doing the wise thing, but you aren't sure which of your options qualifies as the wise choice?

EMOTIONAL STATIC

Wisdom is not always as clear as we would like it to be. There are factors that sometimes cloud our thinking and our judgment. Take emotions, for instance. Emotions are a wonderful thing that God has given us, but emotionally charged situations are not conducive to answering the Best Question Ever.

We have all made decisions in the heat of the moment only to regret them later. Excitement over a person, product, or opportunity will skew our perspective. A good salesperson can engage you emotionally in a product. Emotions can make it hard to see straight, think straight, decide straight. This is almost always the case when love, lust, money, or a crisis is involved—these are not emotionally neutral environments.

Most of the decisions we later regret are made when emotions are running high. My guess is that the decision you regret most was made in an emotionally charged moment: Not only were you unable to identify the wise thing to do, but you didn't really care.

But I love him!

Just look at her!

It's the last one!

It's on sale!

But I've never been invited before!

Emotions can flip on us. Just as we can be emotionally charged about something apparently wonderful, we can find ourselves depressed or angry if circumstances aren't as pleasant. How many times have we found ourselves making a decision in a fit of anger, greed, guilt, loneliness, or jealousy? The truth is, when painful emotions are running high, we don't really care about making wise decisions. We only care about easing the hurt or dishing out the hurt, depending on our situation. It is next to impossible to discern the voice of wisdom when our emotions are raging.

THE KNOW-IT-ALL

Emotions are not the only obstacle when trying to make the wise choice. There are times when we are simply clueless! Because of our lack of experience, our age, or our lack of understanding, we are not able to make the wise choice. And it's tough to fess up to someone—especially your parents—that you aren't sure what to do. But in those times, it is most important to first admit to yourself that you aren't sure where to go or what to do.

Don't feel like this is only an issue for young people. As you get older, the decisions are different, but just as difficult. Eventually, you may end up in a career where people are looking to you for the answers. You're supposed to be the expert. And yet you can't pretend to know it all, because you don't.

So what should you do when you don't know what to do? When you're sweating it out because you want to make the wise choice but you're like a deer in the headlights? Want to know what wise people do in situations like this?

Nothing.

That's it. Wise people do nothing. They don't act. They don't react. They simply do nothing. So how do they end up getting anywhere?

Doing nothing doesn't mean you just sit there.

Wise people know when they *don't know* and are not so foolish as to pretend they *do* know. Eventually they make a decision and move ahead. But only after they have employed their best-kept secret.

KNOWING WHAT YOU DON'T KNOW

THE BEST-KEPT SECRET

Are you ready for the secret to knowing what to do when you don't know what to do and you've decided to do nothing but are ready to do something?

Just this: *Ask someone who does know.*

"Ask someone else? It's that simple? You've got to be kidding me. I need a refund here! There's got to be more to it."

Nope. That's it. It's the best-kept secret of wise men and women everywhere. This is how they became wise, and it is how they continue to appear wise. This is how they manage to make wise decisions concerning areas of specialty in which they have no expertise. This is how they manage to make wise decisions even in emotionally turbulent decision-making environments.

Wise people know when they *don't know*, and they're not afraid to go to those who *do know*. When wise people bump up against their limitations, they stop and ask for help.

When we don't know what to do, we need to go and ask someone who *does* know what to do. Someone who has been there and done that. Someone who is an "expert" in that field. Someone who has been in your shoes before. Someone who can give you that extra boost of wisdom based on their previous experiences.

It may seem a little odd for a wise person to seek wisdom from someone else. After all, what's the use of being wise if you have to ask someone else for the answers? Yet a wise person seeks out wisdom, even if it comes from another source. Because that is the wise thing to do.

In fact, the wisest man ever to walk this earth believed this.

THE WISE GUY

According to the Scriptures, Solomon was the wisest man who ever lived. As a young king, probably in his teen years, he found himself overwhelmed with the responsibilities that befell him. Then one night the Lord appeared to him in a dream and made him a rather unique offer: "Ask what you wish me to give you" (1 Kings 3:5).

Imagine that! What if you had been in Solomon's shoes, and you could have anything in the world just by asking for it. God offered Solomon a blank check and said, "Fill in the amount." Here's how Solomon responded:

> "Now, O LORD my God, You have made Your servant king in place of my father David, yet I am but a little child; I do not know how to go out or come in. Your servant is in the midst of Your people which You have chosen, a great people who are too many to be numbered or counted. So give Your servant an understanding heart to judge Your people to discern between good and evil. For who is able to judge this great people of Yours?" (1 Kings 3:7–9)

What?! Of all the things Solomon could have asked for, he asks for "an understanding heart to judge." I'm sure you would have asked for the same thing. I'm sure *I* would have asked for the same thing. Maybe not. I guess that's why God didn't ask us this question. But Solomon's response was exactly what God was hoping for.

> It was pleasing in the sight of the Lord that Solomon had asked this thing. God said to him, "Because you have asked this thing and have not asked for yourself

long life, nor have asked riches for yourself, nor have you asked for the life of your enemies, but have asked for yourself discernment to understand justice, behold, I have done according to your words. Behold, I have given you a wise and discerning heart, so that there has been no one like you before you, nor shall one like you arise after you. (1 Kings 3:10–12)

And so Solomon was given wisdom and discernment beyond that of any man or woman who had ever lived. He became the go-to guy for just about everything. He was an architect, poet, philosopher, scientist, scholar, theologian, and ruler—a truly amazing individual.

In the New Testament, you and I are encouraged to follow Solomon's example: "If any of you lacks wisdom, he should ask God, who gives generously to all without finding fault, and it will be given to him" (James 1:5, NIV). This wonderful verse contains an important assumption and a powerful promise. The assumption is that there will be times when we don't know the wise thing to do; the promise is that God will provide us with the wisdom we need. But like Solomon, we must first recognize our need.

That leads us to the Best Question Ever. The wisest man who ever lived insists throughout his writings that, instead of looking within our own hearts for the wisdom we need, we should pursue the advice of others. In fact, Solomon had more to say about the importance of seeking advice from wise people than all the other biblical writers combined.

Here is a random sampling:

A wise man will hear and increase in learning, and a man of understanding will acquire wise counsel. (Proverbs 1:5)

The way of a fool is right in his own eyes, but a wise man is he who listens to counsel. (Proverbs 12:15)

Listen to counsel and accept discipline, that you may be wise the rest of your days. (Proverbs 19:20)

Without consultation, plans are frustrated, but with many counselors they succeed. (Proverbs 15:22)

You have to stop and ask yourself why the wisest man in the world would put such a premium on seeking advice from others. The answer, of course, is that he was the wisest man in the world! *Wisdom seeks counsel.* The wise man knows his limitations; it is the fool who believes he has none.

My guess is that Solomon remembered how overwhelmed he felt the day he became king, how badly he needed wisdom beyond his years, how discernment seemed hopelessly out of reach. As wise as he became, Solomon never forgot that his wisdom had come from Someone else. And so even after God granted him extraordinary wisdom,

Solomon continued to surround himself with trusted advisors.

So how about you? Are you willing to ask for advice from someone who might know a little more than you? How about your parents? As much as it might kill you to admit they are right, many times they are. How about other adults—maybe a group leader at church, or even a friend who really wants to help you do the right thing? God can use these people to help you understand what the wise choice is.

LISTENING, LEARNING
THE LONE RANGER WASN'T
REALLY ALONE

Have you ever stopped and thought about the irony of professional athletes' having coaches? Think about it. Why would a guy who can throw a ninety-five-mile-per-hour fastball over the corner of a rubber plate sixty feet and six inches away need advice on how to pitch from an older fellow who may have trouble *seeing* the plate from that far? Why? Because professional athletes know from experience something wise people seem to grasp intuitively.

Every professional athlete knows that he or she will never reach, nor maintain, peak performance apart from outside input. Granted, the superstar pitcher may be the one with the skill, youth, money, and fame. But none of that is enough to keep him performing at his peak. He needs a coach. He needs another set of eyes and another source of insight to help him judge his performance realistically.

Not coincidentally, men and women who consistently make the right moves relationally, professionally, and financially are those who seek input from others. Again, they know what they don't know and aren't afraid to go to those who do know. And this private habit results in very public success.

Incapable and Insufficient

You will never be all you're capable of being unless you tap the wisdom of the wise people around you. Sure, you may get by. You may even do better than most other people. But you will never reach *your full potential* without help and advice from the outside. This is true professionally, spiritually, financially, and even relationally. I say *even* relationally because it can feel so unnatural to seek relational advice, especially at the outset of a relationship.

Think about this. We usually trust our own feelings going into relationships. We listen to emotions and then seek the approval of our friends. Girls, how many times have you fallen for a guy and then asked your friends what they think about him? Guys, you've wooed the new girl into going out with you to homecoming, and then while wearing her on your arm like a trophy, you ask your friends, "So are you impressed or what?"

But what about when those relationships end? We go crying—guys, admit it—to our friends, our parents, whoever will listen. We pour our hearts out and ask, "What do I do?" A little late for that question, don't you think? Think of all the pain and heartache we could have saved ourselves if we would have asked those people that question a little sooner.

If the Best Question Ever is "What is the wise thing for me to do?" then perhaps the second-best question is, "What do *you* think is the wise thing for me to do?" As a parent, there are times I would pay big bucks to get my children to ask me that question and mean it. I'm sure my parents would have paid to get me to ask it as well.

WISE AND WISER

One of the realities of being a preacher's kid is that I grew up hearing stories about the complicated situations people had "behaved" themselves into. Looking back, I realize my dad had an agenda in telling me all those stories. I do the same thing with my kids. If it has the same effect on them as it did on me, then so much the better.

The moral of nearly every one of these stories is, "They

should have listened." People failed because they didn't listen to God, their parents, their friends, or some other voice of reason. Partly as a result of all those stories, I grew up with a healthy respect for sin. Actually, *fear* may be a better description. But I also grew up knowing that it would serve me well to *listen*.

Why not pause long enough to listen to the people who have faced what we're facing, people who have already been through what we're about to go through and are wiser for their experience? Experience *is* a good teacher, especially if it is other people's experience. There's no point in learning something the hard way if someone else has already paid that price.

I am a better husband because of the wise counsel I received before I said, "I do." Sandra and I are much wiser parents as a result of the incredible insights we learned from the men and women we sought counsel from through the years. I know I am a much better leader because of the advice I have received from the seasoned leaders around me. I don't know if it is fear, insecurity, or wisdom, but I just don't make big decisions without outside input. I don't want to find out what I "should have done" after it is too late to do anything about it.

When we receive wise counsel *after* a decision has been made, it is nothing more than a reminder of how wise we could have been had we asked. But let's face it, sometimes we don't want to ask, do we?

MIRROR CHECK

The Bible has a term for the person who refuses wise counsel: *fool*. Solomon summed it up this way: "The way of a fool seems right to him, but a wise man listens to advice" (Proverbs 12:15, NIV). In our culture it sounds harsh to refer to someone as a fool, so we soften it by saying, "He acted foolishly" or, "How could I have been so foolish?" But the reality is, when we refuse to listen, when we dodge the truth, when we insist on having our own way, we are fools.

Wise people know when they don't know. The fool is the person who convinces himself that he knows more than he really knows and doesn't need to ask anybody anything. At the end of the day, the wise man breathes a sigh of relief; the fool, a sigh of regret.

Bottom line, when we resist presenting our options to the wise people around us for fear of hearing what we don't want to hear, we are fools. When we insist on ignoring the warning signs and pressing on anyway, we are fools. And in the end, we pay. Fools always pay.

SOS

God knows there will be times when you lack wisdom, times when you will ask the Best Question Ever and come up short.

If you are in the midst of an emotionally challenging situation and circumstances require you to make a decision, go for help. Don't trust your judgment alone. Just as there are times when physical pain makes us incapable of caring for ourselves, so emotional pain can drive us to the place where we need assistance.

If you are being called upon to make a decision that is out of your league in terms of experience or education, get some help. Don't pretend. Don't fake it. Asking for help is not a reflection of your lack of wisdom. Asking for input is *evidence of* wisdom. When the Best Question Ever doesn't yield the clarity you need, ask somebody you trust, "In light of my past experience, current circumstances, and future hopes and dreams, what do *you* believe is the wise thing for me to do?"

After all, wise people know when they don't know and aren't afraid to go to those who do.

WALK WITH THE WISE
THE POWER OF FRIENDSHIP

Growing up I remember making some good choices and some bad choices. I remember making choices that I later regretted and choices that I was excited about. When I think back to those times, I remember certain faces that were there with me. I remember friends I talked with about my decisions and the advice that they gave me. And my decisions were usually heavily influenced by the people I surrounded myself with. Sometimes I would even change my mind about what to do based on what my friends told me.

Let's face it, we need people. God has made us to desire relationships and friendships. Even in preschool, we start calling other kids our friends and playing with them. Later we form cliques and begin to hang out with people with whom we have something in common. Even as adults, friendships can have a powerful influence in our lives. It's all part of the design.

TAKE A WALK

I enjoy walking along the beach. There's something about the shoreline that I find peaceful and relaxing. I often like to walk alone, but there are times when I prefer to walk with someone else. And when we get back, I know whether or not it was a good walk based on the person I walked with. If he or she talked too much or complained about the sand in their toes or said it was too hot or too cold—bad walk. But if my companion talked and listened and noticed the seagulls flying overhead or pointed out a cool sandcastle—good walk. Why is the success or failure of my walk determined by the actions of someone else? Because they influenced my experience.

The friends in our life can deeply affect our life experiences. I'm not saying your friends have to look for seagulls or notice sandcastles, but they will influence many of the decisions you make, for better or worse. I think Proverbs says this best:

He who walks with the wise grows wise, but a companion of fools suffers harm. (Proverbs 13:20, NIV)

There's that word again, *fool*. It seems there is a pattern here for those who ignore the path that leads to wisdom. Those who surround themselves with "fools" will suffer harm. I'm not making this stuff up, folks—it's right there! But I probably don't have to convince you of this truth.

Think back to the time when you made an unwise decision. One that you regretted later. One that caused you and/or your loved ones pain when all was said and done. Who was there with you when you made that choice? Who influenced your decision? Were the people you surrounded yourself with concerned about doing the right thing or just living for the pleasure of the moment? Odds are, they weren't overly concerned with making the wise choice. And who paid for it later? You did.

If you walk through life with people who are pursuing the same values as you are, then your decisions concerning such issues as time, money, and morality will be made a whole lot easier. But if you surround yourself with companions who are not concerned with making wise choices and are focused on other things in life, then you will find that wise decisions are very difficult to make.

There's a phrase we use with students at our church that helps them remember this principle. It goes something like this: *Your friends will determine the direction and quality of your life.*

If you want to exercise wisdom in your dating life, hang out with people who are wise about dating. If you want to be wise in your moral life, hang out with people who live morally. If you want to spend your time wisely, don't hang out with people who seem to be wasting their lives away.

Take a hard, honest look at your friends. Are they wise? Or are they foolish? Before you worry about making wise choices, worry about who your friends are. You will need the everyday support of wise friends in order to ask and respond to the Best Question Ever.

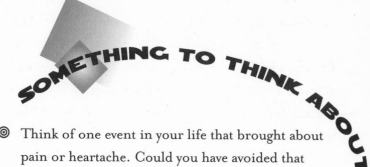

SOMETHING TO THINK ABOUT

◎ Think of one event in your life that brought about pain or heartache. Could you have avoided that pain if you had asked someone else what you should do?

◎ Do you find it difficult to ask someone else for help? Why or why not?

◎ Can you ask your parents for help? Why or why not?

◎ Why is it important to ask someone else when you aren't sure what the wise choice is?

◎ Are the friends you currently have concerned with making wise choices in life? If not, what can you do to change that?

PART VI

THE BEST DECISION EVER

PERFECTING YOUR FOLLOW-THROUGH

PAINTING INSIDE THE LINES

In light of your past experience, current circumstances, and future hopes and dreams, what is the wise thing for you to do? What do the wise people around you consider the wisest course of action for you to take? These are two extraordinarily powerful questions that you should bring to bear on every area of your life. Acting on the answers to these questions will set you up to live a life of few regrets.

But therein lies the problem: *You have to act.* You have to follow through. For your heavenly Father to leverage the Best Question Ever in your life, you have to act on what you discover. In these final pages I want to help position you for follow-through.

THE GALLERY

Several years ago, toward the end of a long day alone with the kids, Sandra marched everybody to the basement and announced that they were to spend the afternoon painting. She covered a big table with butcher paper, pulled out three small canvases, laid out assorted paints and brushes, and told them that *she* would let *them* know when they were finished!

"Paint what?" asked Andrew, who was nine at the time.

"Anything you please."

"I don't know what to paint," said Allie, who was seven.

"I don't even know *how* to paint," complained Garrett, who was eight.

Without giving further instructions, Sandra headed back upstairs for a well-deserved nap. Thirty minutes later she was awakened by a sound that she rarely heard: silence. No voices. No make-believe explosions. No crying. Nothing. The house was quiet.

Concerned, she headed down the hall to the basement door. No sooner had she opened the door when she heard, "Don't come down yet—we aren't finished." In mom-speak that meant, "Go have a few moments for yourself," an offer Sandra gladly accepted. Twenty short minutes later she heard the pitter-patter of six precious feet scrambling up the basement stairs. "We're ready! We're ready! Come see our artwork!"

What kind of paintings do you suppose were waiting for Sandra at the bottom of the stairs? What kind of art would you expect from three untrained, unattended young children? Three masterpieces? Three introspective self-portraits worthy of hanging in a local gallery?

Why not?

Why is it you imagine unintelligible strokes of paint splattered all over the canvases, the table, and the basement floor? Why are your expectations so low when it comes to my children's artwork?

There's a whole list of reasons. What it all boils down to, however, is that untrained artists won't make the right decisions. Untrained artists don't know the principles and guidelines of painting. They don't know proper technique. Their motives may be pure and their intent noble, but if they don't know how to paint—well, you get the picture.

PLAYING BY THE RULES

We all know there are certain rules in this world that we have to abide by. There are rules that your teachers have set up to run your classroom. If you go against the rules, you might end up headed to the principal's office. If you play by the rules, your chances of getting a good grade in the class are a whole lot better. Rules are there to help keep us in line, to provide some structure for the way we work and play.

For the last four years I have been a coach or an assistant coach for my sons' baseball teams. I learned very quickly that knowing the rules and understanding the nuances of Little League baseball make all the difference in a coach's decision-making ability.

For example, in our league there is a five-run limit rule. That is, once a team scores five runs in an inning, their turn at bat is over and the other team automatically comes up to bat. In the sixth and final inning, there are no run limits; however, because of a time limit imposed on Little League games, very few of our games ever make it to the sixth inning.

In spite of the run-limit rule, the coaches in our league typically arrange their batting orders the traditional way—that is, they arrange their lineup so that all their best hitters bat first and all their worst hitters bat at the end of the lineup. But one day it occurred to me that under the circumstances they had it all wrong. If there is a five-run limit each inning, that changes the goal of the game. The goal should be to score five runs *every inning*. So I started arranging our batting order accordingly. Instead of putting our worst batters at the bottom of the order, I sprinkled them throughout the lineup.

Suddenly, we started scoring consistently every inning. And as a result of moving the weaker batters up in the order, something else happened in our favor: The weaker batters started hitting. Moving them up in the order did something for their confidence. We won more games that season than any team in the league.

You see, knowing the way things work makes you a better decision-maker. Every decision may not be obvious, but knowing the rules and principles narrows our options and increases our chances of success. It gives us a better chance to win.

IT CUTS BOTH WAYS

Generally speaking, when we ignore the rules or principles governing any particular field, we pay a price. Recently we saw one of the worst sports brawls ever at an NBA game. Even if you're not into basketball, you saw it on the news or at least heard someone talking about it. It's one thing to have a fight among players on the court, but it's another to take it into the stands. There are rules in the game concerning both events. Fighting on the court might deserve a penalty, but when a player goes into the stands there's a much bigger price to pay. And in this case, there were some pretty heavy fines and suspensions. Were the players sorry? Sure, but they still had to pay the price for breaking the rules.

This is why people who represent themselves in court usually don't fare very well. They don't know the law. They don't understand courtroom etiquette. They have no experience picking or reading a jury. They don't know the first thing about cross-examining a witness.

That's why when it's time to go to court it makes sense to hire someone else to represent you—someone who has attended law school and knows the law and how to defend it. You don't want to place your legal standing in the hands of some guy off the street who just likes to argue.

HANDS ON

Knowing the rules and principles of a particular discipline is not enough. To harness their power, you must submit to or apply them. When a surgeon performs an operation, he is submitting to the rules and applying the procedures of his particular specialty. No matter how skilled his hands, if he were to ignore proper surgical procedures, the results could be devastating.

Wide receivers can't cut out around the cheerleaders, come back onto the field, and catch a pass without being penalized. LeBron James can't jump off the bench and rip the goal down with a slam dunk without first checking into the game. The Atlanta Braves can't put ten players on the field at a time. Professional athletes must submit to the rules in order to win.

In every field it is both the knowing and the doing that

makes for success. You must first know how things work and then submit yourself to those principles, laws, and techniques. It is what you know and what you do with what you know that make the difference.

So...

THE BEGINNING
OF WISDOM
AN ACT OF SURRENDER

What's true in the realms of medicine, construction, accounting, and sports is true in the core dimensions of your life as well. There are laws and principles that must be adhered to if you are to succeed in any area of life—relationships, finances, school, work, or time management. Knowing and submitting to these principles will make all the difference in the world. For it is within the context of these life rules that wisdom is found. They inform the decision-making process.

Every time you give someone advice, you are drawing upon your insight about how some aspect of the world works. Through the years you have stumbled onto some of these laws and principles. Some you have learned the hard way. You may have been exposed to others through the wisdom of your parents and teachers. But you know a thing or two about how life works. There are certain bad decisions you can spot a mile away. You can see trouble coming. At times you have tried to warn some unsuspecting soul to get out of the way—just like somebody warned you in a previous chapter of your life.

With all of this experience as a backdrop, let me ask you a couple of questions. If I can't expect my children to create a masterpiece on canvas when they do not know and submit to the rules and principles of oil painting, how can we expect to make a masterpiece of our lives without knowing and submitting to the laws and principles of life? If I can't expect my mechanic to make wise decisions about the maintenance of my car without first knowing how the car works, how can I expect to make wise decisions about my family and finances without first knowing the laws and principles that govern these important arenas of life?

Let me take it one excruciating step further. How do you expect to make a masterpiece of your life if you are unwilling to surrender to the Author of life—the One who knows which textures and colors are best blended for the outcome you desire? How do you expect to make wise decisions regarding your family, your love life, your education, and career if you are not willing to submit to the promptings of the One who knows more about those things than you or I ever will?

IN THE BEGINNING

Perhaps it was this line of reasoning that led the wisest man in the world to pen these words: "The fear of the LORD is the beginning of wisdom" (Proverbs 9:10). Wisdom begins with a proper understanding of who God is and who we are not.

Don't rush past this too quickly. Throughout this book I have challenged you to ask *yourself*, "What is the wise thing for me to do?" In the previous section I encouraged you to broaden your audience to a few choice and respected friends. But to fully leverage the Best Question Ever, you need to address it to your heavenly Father. For He is the source of all wisdom, and wisdom begins by properly aligning ourselves with who God is.

Solomon uses the phrase the "the fear of the Lord." In this context, "fear" refers to recognition and reverence that leads to submission. You may want to write that down somewhere. Wisdom begins with the *recognition* of who God is. This does not mean simply recognizing His power and knowledge. This is recognizing that you are dealing with the one and only Creator of all things. God with a capital *G*. Wisdom begins when we rightly recognize God's position as God!

Proper recognition results in *reverence*. Reverence is the appropriate response to the One who created and controls all things. The practical side of reverence is submission. Those who recognize and revere the Father have little choice but to embrace His right to rule all that He has created. That moment of recognition and surrender is the beginning of true wisdom.

Lest we lose sight of the highly relational side of our heavenly Father, Solomon restates his point in different terms. Here's how the entire verse reads:

> The fear of the LORD is the beginning of wisdom, and the knowledge of the Holy One is understanding. (Proverbs 9:10)

Allow me to paraphrase this amazing verse for you this way:

> Wisdom begins when we recognize that God is God and then respond accordingly. The proper response, of course, is surrender. Once we have surrendered, God is more than happy to reveal more and more of Himself.

And as we discover more and more of who God is, we begin to get a better picture of the world He created, including us. As we understand more, we grow in our ability to choose wisely. So true wisdom begins with a proper understanding of who God is followed by a proper response—surrender.

If the idea of surrendering to your heavenly Father scares you, consider this: You unknowingly surrender to His principles and laws every day. Every time you make a wise decision about a date, you are applying or surrendering to one of God's principles. Every time you make a wise decision about what to do with your time, the same thing is true. Every time you submit your body to the knife of a competent surgeon, you surrender yourself to the laws of God. The surgeon is simply making decisions based upon his understanding of the way God created the human body. Every time you submit to a human authority, you are applying one of God's principles.

"But that's different," you argue. "I'm just using good judgment." That may be the way you see it. But if you are simply applying principles that existed before you chose to apply them, you are borrowing from—and recognizing the wisdom of—the Father. Think about it. We have discovered and leveraged principles of physics; we have explored and manipulated the genetic code; we have pinpointed and eradicated many diseases. Our forefathers harnessed high- and low-pressure systems and used them to travel across the seas. (All of the things that might bore you in school but have changed the world we live in.)

Every single day we benefit from the way God designed things to work. Everything we claim to have created in our human endeavors finds its ultimate source in something God created that we simply discovered and manipulated. Every time we take a breath, we declare our dependency upon and submission to the Father physically. Why then would we hesitate to submit our will? Why are we so afraid to surrender to Him our relationships, our money, and our future?

A wise physician does not ignore the way God created the body. A wise pilot does not ignore the law of gravity. The beginning of wisdom is recognition of and submission to the One who designed things to work the way things work.

IT'S MUTUAL

One more thought on surrender: It is mutual. Mutual surrender, or submission if you prefer, is one of the most powerful relational dynamics. When two people pledge to put the other first, that is relationship at its best. This is true whether we're talking about a husband and wife, teacher and student, employee and employer, or parent and child. In a relationship of mutual submission, rank and birth order are irrelevant. The point is that each has pledged all that he or she is for the benefit of the other. In a relationship of mutual submission, there is nothing to fear—it is a relationship of trust.

Here's a bit of truth that ought to erase all your misgivings about surrendering to the Father: Before you were born, He submitted Himself to you. On a wooden cross, God sacrificed His best on your behalf. He put you ahead of Himself. Read these words with that thought in mind:

You see, at just the right time, when we were still powerless, Christ died for the ungodly. Very rarely will anyone die for a righteous man, though for a good man someone might possibly dare to die. But

God demonstrates his own love for us in this: While we were still sinners, Christ died for us. (Romans 5:6–8, NIV)

While you had nothing to offer, Christ died for you. He put your sin ahead of His own glory. In this way, He submitted to you. He met your greatest need at great personal expense. To do so, did He demonstrate His authority? No. His right to rule? Nope. Instead, He drew from His vast resources to demonstrate the only thing that would give us the courage to submit fearlessly, courageously: He demonstrated His love. And that demonstration stands as an open invitation for us to respond in kind. And so we are called into a relationship of mutual submission, knowing all the while that our Father took the risk and went first. He made the first move even though He didn't have to.

I know from my own experience that it is far easier to *believe in* than to *surrender to* God. It's easier to ask myself the Best Question Ever than it is to sincerely ask this question of the Father. But the cross stands as a constant reminder that I have nothing to fear. God can be trusted. After all, He has already demonstrated His unconditional love for me.

THE BEST OF THE BEST

In the end it all comes down to this. Our willingness to ask and respond to the Best Question Ever depends upon our willingness to make the *best decision ever*—the decision to fully submit our lives to our heavenly Father. This is where wisdom begins.

What's true of my children in the realm of art is true of all of us in our lives, relationships, and finances. We know all too well what happens when we paint on our own, when we wave God off in order to choose our own colors, strokes, and textures. Each of us carries the scars, the memories, and the regrets of those seasons when we listened to our will before His.

God desires that your life be a masterpiece that reflects His greatness and your uniqueness. But to create a masterpiece with our lives, we must submit ourselves to the hand of the Master. We must allow Him to influence each stroke on the canvas of our lives.

So let me ask you, Have you made the best decision ever? Have you fully surrendered all of you to all of Him? Have you pre-decided to submit to His will before you know what He will ask? If not, I can't think of a more appropriate way to end our time together than to give you an opportunity to pray a prayer of surrender. There's nothing special about these words. It is the attitude of your heart that will make the difference.

Heavenly Father, today I place myself

under Your authority.

I surrender all of me to You.

As You demonstrated Your love

for me through the death of Your Son,

so I desire to demonstrate my love for You

through a renewed mind and surrendered will.

Your will be done in me.

I surrender all.

In the name of my Savior, I pray.

Amen.

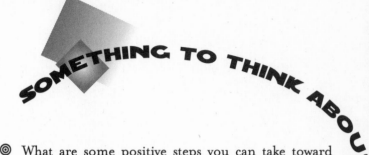

SOMETHING TO THINK ABOUT

◎ What are some positive steps you can take toward knowing how to consistently make the wise choice?

◎ Can you truly make the wise choice without God in you life?

◎ What areas of your life have you not surrendered to God?

◎ Is it easier to make the wise choice in areas you have surrendered to Him or in those you have not surrendered?

◎ Write down the areas of your life you have not surrendered to God but want Him to take control of from now on.

Am I Good Enough?
by Andy Stanley

1-59052-467-5

In this updated edition of the bestselling book, *How Good Is Good Enough?* teen readers find out why Jesus taught that goodness is not even a requirement to enter heaven—and why Christianity is beyond fair.

Louder than Words
by Andy Stanley

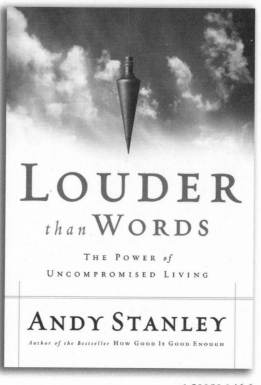

1-59052-346-6

Sharing a life-changing strategy for personal character development, Andy Stanley helps you determine your own definition of success and introduces a step-by-step program for prioritizing your life, overcoming barriers, and more.